Getting into Words

Getting into Words

Vocabulary Instruction that Strengthens Comprehension

by

Shira Lubliner, Ed.D.

with

Linda Smetana, Ed.D.

Teacher Education Department
California State University, Hayward

·PAUL·H·
BROOKES
PUBLISHING Co.®

Baltimore • London • Sydney

Paul H. Brookes Publishing Co.
Post Office Box 10624
Baltimore, Maryland 21285-0624

www.brookespublishing.com

Manufactured in the United States of America by
Edwards Brothers, Lillington, North Carolina.

Permission is gratefully acknowledged to use the graphics/images appearing in this
publication courtesy of Art Explosion © 1995–2001 Nova Development Corporation
and its licensors and ClickArt® Incredible Image Pak © 1999 Mattel, Inc. and its
licensors. All rights reserved.

The extract on page 35 is from AMERICA WILL BE in HOUGHTON MIFFLIN
SOCIAL STUDIES by Armento, et al. Copyright © 1991 by Houghton Mifflin Company. Reprinted by permission of Houghton Mifflin Company. All rights reserved.

The extract on page 139 is from THE DAY THE GOOSE GOT LOOSE by Reeve
Lindbergh, copyright © 1990 by Reeve Lindbergh. Used by permission of Dial Books
for Young Readers, A Division of Penguin Young Readers Group. A Member of Penguin Group (USA) Inc., 345 Hudson Street, New York, NY 10014. All rights reserved.

The vignettes in this book are composites based on the authors' experiences. In most
instances, names and identifying details have been changed to protect confidentiality.
In all other cases, individuals' names and stories are used by permission.

All photographs in this book and on the cover are used by permission of the individuals pictured or their parents or guardians.

Library of Congress Cataloging-in-Publication Data

Lubliner, Shira, 1951–
    Getting into words : vocabulary instruction that strengthens comprehension / by
Shira Lubliner; with Linda Smetana.
        p.   cm.
    Includes bibliographical references and index.
    ISBN 1-55766-789-6 (layflat pbk.)
    1. Vocabulary—Study and teaching (Elementary)   I. Smetana, Linda Diane.
    II. Title.

LB1574.5.L83 2005
372.61—dc22   2004015576

British Library Cataloguing in Publication data are available from the British Library.

Contents

About the Authors

Shira Lubliner, Ed.D., Assistant Professor, Teacher Education Department, California State University, Hayward, 25800 Carlos Bee Boulevard, Hayward, CA 94542

Shira Lubliner has been an educator for more than 30 years, working as a classroom teacher, a private school principal, and a teacher educator. She taught a variety of grade levels, working with children in elementary school, middle school, and high school. After many years as an administrator, Dr. Lubliner returned to the classroom to teach fifth grade in a diverse California public school.

Dr. Lubliner completed her doctorate in learning and instruction at the University of San Francisco and is currently an assistant professor of teacher education at California State University, Hayward. She teaches methods classes for preservice teachers and graduate reading courses and conducts classroom-based research in local elementary schools.

Shira Lubliner's research interests focus on methods of vocabulary instruction that improve children's reading comprehension achievement. She designed a comprehensive program of vocabulary development, on which this book is based, that can be implemented by classroom teachers using regular instructional materials. Results from a recent study she conducted in one of California's lowest performing Title I schools documented large gains in vocabulary and reading comprehension and a narrowing of the achievement gap between Title I students and those in an above-average school following the implementation of this comprehensive vocabulary development program (Lubliner & Smetana, 2004, manuscript submitted for publication).

Dr. Lubliner presents workshops for teachers on vocabulary instruction and reading comprehension throughout the United States and is often a speaker at the annual meetings of the American Educational Research Association, the International Reading Association, the National Council for the Social Studies, and the California Reading Association. Dr. Lubliner is the author of the article "Help for Struggling Upper-Grade Elementary Readers" (*The Reading Teacher,* February 2004) and the book *A Practical Guide to Reciprocal Teaching* (Wright Group/McGraw-Hill, 2001).

Shira Lubliner has been married to Efi Lubliner for 29 years and is the mother of four delightful children, Dania, Leora, Dori, and Elan Lubliner.

Linda Smetana, Ed.D., Assistant Professor, Teacher Education Department, California State University, Hayward, 25800 Carlos Bee Boulevard, Hayward, CA 94542

Linda Smetana has worked as an educator for more than 30 years. She taught in the public school system from kindergarten through continuation high school. Since the 1980s, her work has centered on strategies for students with reading difficulties and learning disabilities. She teaches courses in reading, language arts, and special education at California State University, Hayward. Her current research and teaching interests are fluency and vocabulary development and application of such strategies in classroom settings.

Linda Smetana has been married for 33 years to Ron Smetana and is the mother of Daniel and Joel Smetana.

Acknowledgments

Many people contributed to the publication of this book. I would like to acknowledge my colleague Linda Smetana, who shared my conviction that vocabulary instruction is an essential factor in children's academic achievement. Linda provided a great deal of help with the research that underlies this book, wrote the glossary, and was a constant source of support.

I would also like to acknowledge the public school teachers who helped bring this book to life. Many thanks to Rhona Wanetick, Lynne Cheney, Martha Thomas, Rachel Sterrett, and Amy Johnson for their wonderful work. They graciously invited me into their classrooms, shared their students with me, skillfully implemented my recommendations, and provided thoughtful feedback regarding the methods and materials that are included in this book. I offer special thanks to Vicki Eversole and Jana Perkins, graduates of the Reading Specialist Program at California State University, Hayward. Vicki and Jana worked with me on their master's theses, examining the effects of vocabulary instruction on students' reading comprehension. Their work provided me with rich research opportunities and a chance to document the effectiveness of *Getting Into Words* in the real world of diverse public school classrooms. I learned much from my teachers and a great deal from my colleagues, but I learned most of all from my students!

Special thanks to Jessica Allan, Mika Sam Smith, and Amy Kopperude, my editors at Paul H. Brookes Publishing Co., for their thoughtful guidance throughout the process of preparing the manuscript for publication. They were a delight to work with and helped transform my manuscript into a book to be proud of.

Finally, I'd like to thank my husband, Efi Lubliner, for his patience with my absorption in this undertaking and his pride in my accomplishments. I couldn't have done it without him!

To our children:
Dania, Leora, Dori, and Elan Lubliner
and
Daniel and Joel Smetana

Part I

Getting Started

Introduction

It was a bright fall morning—the first day of school. The bell rang and the teacher opened the classroom door and smiled at 34 expectant faces. She welcomed the children with a familiar sense of excitement, imagining miraculous growth in every young mind. All things seem possible on the first day of school!

The teacher loved "getting into words," probing for nuances of meaning in texts and finding just the right words to express herself in writing. She understood the importance of vocabulary and prepared carefully for the moment that she would initiate the children into the world of words. She was determined to ignite their imaginations with and inspire them to "get into words," too. The teacher opened the poetry book and spoke softly to children before beginning to read: "I want you to close your eyes and listen carefully as I read this poem. Let the author paint a picture in your mind.

The wind was a torrent of darkness among the gusty trees,
The moon was a ghostly galleon tossed upon cloudy seas,
The road was a ribbon of moonlight over the purple moor,
And the highwayman came riding—
   Riding—riding—
The highwayman came riding up to the old inn-door.
(From "The Highwayman," Alfred Noyes, 1907, p. 35)

"Now, open your eyes and read the first verse of the poem again yourself. Picture the scene the author is describing. Then take your pastels and draw the picture that you see in your mind."

The children concentrated, completely absorbed by the task. The teacher walked around quietly as the pictures emerged. Many of the children drew ships, having inferred the meaning of the word *galleon* from context. Although none of the children could define *highwayman*, most had understood enough to draw a horseman. The words came to life in pastel colors; yes, the students understood the poem!

A few days later the children were working on their own writing. Alex had written a poem about a falcon, but the words were dull and lifeless. He was frustrated with the teacher's comments: "Alex, you've come up with a good sketch in this poem, but I can't see your falcon in my imagination. You need powerful words to paint a picture I can read and see in my mind."

"I don't know words like that," Alex countered. "How am I supposed to use words I don't even know?"

"Hmm....Let's figure this out. How could you find stronger words for your poem?"

"You could tell me!" Alex suggested hopefully.

"But that won't work very often, Alex. You'll need words when I'm not around or when I'm helping other kids. We need to find a way for you to be an independent word learner. Where could you find words about falcons?"

"In a book?"

"Great idea!" The teacher replied. "We have some reference books on the shelf. I think there's a book about birds of prey."

Alex found the book and located a section about falcons. He read a description of the falcon's talons. He quickly replaced the word *claws* in his poem with *talons,* a word that he had not known. The teacher praised his efforts and urged him to continue reading about falcons. The poem improved dramatically as Alex read and learned vivid words that brought his ideas to life. His enthusiasm soared as the poem took shape. Alex proudly read his poem, titled "Five Ways to Look at a Falcon," aloud to his classmates, who assured him that they could picture the falcon in their minds:

> *The falcon ready to trap its prey with mighty talons*
> *The falcon with its graceful dive, aiming for its enemy....*

While I was writing *Getting Into Words: Vocabulary Instruction that Strengthens Comprehension,* I was inspired by many of the children I taught and the experiences I had as a fifth-grade teacher. Linda Smetana assisted me with the book, adding her experiences and insights to this endeavor. Now a professor of teacher education, I work closely with educators and know that they have the daunting responsibility of transmitting an everincreasing body of knowledge and skills to children of the 21st century. Raised on sound bites and video games, many of these youngsters enter our classrooms with little interest in reading and a very limited vocabulary. Teaching lists of words is not going to provide children with the keys to literacy. Children who see only dreary gray in books must be initiated into the world of words, a world filled with light and color. Motivating children to "get into" words

entails much more than conventional vocabulary instruction. It involves creating a purpose for word learning. When children are touched by beautifully written poetry and prose, they are willing to wrestle with these texts to extract meaning. When they are inspired to write beautifully, they search for just the right word to express their own thoughts. Just as they need inspiration to become engaged in word-learning activities, children must be taught the tools of success. They need to learn effective strategies and metacognitive skills so that they can take charge of their own learning. Teaching children to get into words launches them on their way to academic success. I hope that this book will be your guide as you seek to initiate children into the world of words.

Chapter 1

The Tools of Success

I often think of children such as Ashley, Todd, Hernando, and Stacey, the students who did not succeed in my classroom. Ashley was a lively girl who seemed to enjoy school. She read fluently but did not understand anything that she read. Todd was quiet and withdrawn. He resisted reading and read so little that he made minimal progress from year to year. Hernando started school speaking only Spanish. Though he worked on his assignments with fierce determination, lack of English proficiency limited his achievement. Stacey had a chaotic childhood prior to her placement in foster care and did not start school until she was in first grade. Although she tried hard to do well in school, Stacey was so far behind that she never caught up with her peers. Ashley, Todd, Hernando, and Stacey were struggling readers. They passed through my classroom and needed more help than I was able to give them at the time.

I began my work in vocabulary development in response to the needs of children such as these four. I was concerned about my students' poor reading skills but did not realize at the time that vocabulary was the source of the problem. My inquiry began with the reading comprehension literature, as I searched for ideas that might help struggling readers. I learned that cognitive strategies and self-regulation had been shown to improve reading comprehension proficiency (Gambrell, Morrow, Neuman, & Pressley, 1999; Palincsar, 1983, 1985; Pearson & Dole, 1987; Pressley et al., 1995; Rosenshine, 1997). I taught my students to use strategies and to monitor their own comprehension while reading. These methods worked well, and I was pleased with the progress of most of the children. I noticed, however, that some children, particularly those from disadvantaged families, did not seem to benefit from this instruction. When I examined their reading performance more closely, I realized that struggling readers could not use comprehension strategies effectively because they did not know enough words to make sense of the texts. Surprisingly, many of the average students also showed signs of vocabulary-related reading problems. They did not transfer word knowledge from vocabulary instruction to books and were unable to manage word-learning tasks. These problems limited the students' ability to construct meaning when confronted by challenging texts.

I tried to envision an instructional program that would provide the children with the vocabulary they needed. But the problem was immense. Vocabulary experts estimate that children need to learn 3,000 words per year (Baumann, Kame'enui, & Ash, 2003; Nagy & Herman, 1984). Instructional time is limited, and, realistically, teachers can only explicitly teach 300–400 words during a school year. Children acquire most new vocabulary through reading, but many low-performing students are resistant to reading and read very little outside of class. Despite my best efforts, the vocabulary gap was growing wider. It became clear that my students needed better vocabulary instruction and greater reading volume. Unless their vocabulary development could be accelerated, my low-performing students were likely to fall further and further behind.

I reviewed the report of the National Reading Panel (NRP; National Institute of Child Health and Human Development, 2000; see also Kamil, 2004) and found comprehension strategies that could be adapted to increase word-learning proficiency. For example, the NRP identified mental imagery as a strategy that improves reading comprehension proficiency. I used this method to boost children's imaginations and to help them construct the meaning of words, as illustrated in the first vignette in the Introduction. When I asked the children to create a mental image of the line "the moon was a ghostly galleon, tossed upon cloudy seas" (Noyes, 1907, p. 35), they spontaneously implemented word-learning strategies to make sense of the word *galleon*. In addition to using mental imagery, I adapted several other methods of increasing comprehension of texts, such as self-generated questioning, predicting, and comprehension monitoring, to build word-learning skills. Comprehension monitoring, a method with an extensive research base (NRP, 2000), was particularly effective. When children were taught to monitor their comprehension of words and to self-regulate word learning, they developed independent word-learning skills and their reading comprehension improved. The Tools of Success (described later in this chapter) were beginning to take shape!

When I became a professor of teacher education, I identified key research findings that shaped my thinking about vocabulary acquisition and instruction. The instructional methods contained in this book are based on the following foundational beliefs:

- Vocabulary knowledge is closely related to reading comprehension and academic achievement (Chall, Jacobs, & Baldwin, 1990; Graves, 2000).

- Vocabulary limitations (particularly those of disadvantaged children) are a major factor in the achievement gap (Biemiller, 1999, 2004; Chall et al., 1990; Hart & Risley, 1995, 1999).

- Rich, in-depth vocabulary instruction fosters vocabulary growth that has a positive impact on reading comprehension (Beck, McKeown, & Kucan, 2002; Nagy, Anderson, & Herman, 1987; Stahl & Fairbanks, 1986).

- Repeated exposures to new words is an important source of vocabulary growth (Baumann et al., 2003; Nagy, 1985, 1988; Nagy & Herman 1984).

- Most vocabulary is acquired incidentally during reading, so increasing reading volume is an important factor in accelerating vocabulary development (Nagy et al., 1987; Nagy & Herman, 1984; Stanovich 1986; Swanborn & de Glopper, 1999).

- Incidental word learning during reading is inefficient, but children can be taught intentional word-learning skills that increase the efficiency of vocabulary acquisition (Baumann et al., 2003; Nagy, 1985, 1988).

- Effective vocabulary instruction is based on a combination of procedural knowledge (strategies), conditional knowledge (self-monitoring and self-regulation), and declarative word knowledge (explicit instruction of words that children need to know) (Ruddell, 1994).

- Use of word-learning strategies such as derivation of word meaning from context and structural analysis helps children become independent word learners (Baumann et al., 2003; Nagy, 1985, 1988).

- Teaching children self-regulating skills encourages them to monitor comprehension and to take charge of their own word learning and comprehension (Graves, 1997, 2000; Palincsar, 1983, 1985).

- Effective vocabulary instruction that begins in the primary grades can help narrow the achievement gap between children of differing socioeconomic groups (Biemiller, 1999, 2004).

CONCEPTUAL MODEL

Once I identified the foundational beliefs about vocabulary acquisition and instruction, I turned to the question of reading comprehension. I knew from my experience as a teacher that vocabulary is closely related to reading comprehension. But it was important to gain an understanding of the factors that contribute to vocabulary acquisition and how vocabulary knowledge influences and is influenced by reading comprehension. A review of the research literature indicated that a number of factors influence vocabulary and reading comprehension proficiency; however, the causal relationships are not fully understood (Baumann et al., 2003). The conceptual model in Figure 1.1 clarifies the relationship between the factors linking vocabulary and reading comprehension.

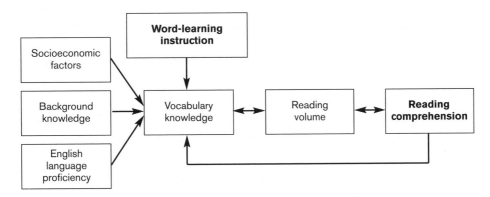

Figure 1.1. Conceptual model of the factors that mediate the influence of vocabulary on reading comprehension.

The conceptual model demonstrates that socioeconomic factors, background knowledge, and English language proficiency affect vocabulary knowledge, which influences and is influenced by reading volume and reading comprehension proficiency. Word-learning instruction, however, mediates the influence of factors limiting vocabulary knowledge. When vocabulary knowledge improves, it sets a circular pattern into motion. Children read more, comprehend more, learn more words, and do better in school. Effective word-learning instruction is the key to launching the upward spiral that leads to academic success (see Chapter 11 for further discussion).

TRADITIONAL VOCABULARY INSTRUCTION THAT DOES NOT WORK

Vocabulary instruction appears to have changed little over the past several decades. Children are given word lists and are taught to look up words in the dictionary, use them in sentences, and memorize the definitions. Unfortunately, there is little evidence that these definitional methods are effective in accelerating children's vocabulary growth (McKeown, 1993).

Go Look it Up

What is your earliest memory of vocabulary instruction? Perhaps you remember encountering an unknown word during reading and asking a teacher or parent what the word meant. "Go look it up" was the inevitable reply. You may remember the frustration that ensued, particularly if you tried to follow your teacher's or parent's instructions.

Imagine that you, a proficient adult reader, are reading a text and encounter the word *pedunculate.* You remember the instructions you were given as a child and look it up in the dictionary. The definition tells you that *pedunculate* means having a peduncle (Stein, 1975). You look up the word *peduncle* and find that it is a stalk that bears flowers or the fructification in fungi. You may still not be sure what the word *pedunculate* means, 5 minutes have elapsed, and you have probably forgotten the content of the text passage. In addition, you have encountered several more challenging words such as *stalk, fructification,* and *fungi* that add to the complexity of the word-learning task.

Children's dictionaries are not much better. If you were to ask your students to look up the word *aristocrat* in the *Macmillan Dictionary for Children* (Levey, 1989) they would find the following definition: a person who is a member of the aristocracy. Once again, the dictionary does not provide much help in determining word meaning. As in the case of the adult dictionary, the children's dictionary complicates the quest for word meaning because the definitions contain complex words that children may not understand.

When a child is reading silently, asks for help with an unknown word, and is told, "Go look it up," he is likely to be frustrated. He is engaged with a text and just wants to know the meaning of the word so he can continue reading. The command "Go look it up" breaks his concentration, interfering with comprehension. He may have difficulty finding the unknown word, particularly if it has an inflected ending (e.g., *-ed, -s, -es, -ing*) or suffix. For example, the child may not realize that the dictionary definition for *establish* is appropriate if he is looking up the word *establishing*. Once he successfully locates the word in the dictionary, he may have to choose among several definitions. The child may also find that he does not understand the definition any more than the original word. At this point the child's reading experience has been completely disrupted and no vocabulary acquisition has occurred. The advice "go look it up" has been completely counterproductive.

Use it in a Sentence

Another common form of vocabulary acquisition instruction is assigning children the task of writing sentences with the new words. Several factors make this activity difficult for children: 1) limited understanding of the words, 2) limited conceptual knowledge about the words, 3) limited syntactical knowledge in reference to the words. When a proficient adult reader tries to formulate a meaningful sentence with the word *pedunculate,* she begins to appreciate the difficulty of this task. The dictionary definition, "having a peduncle," provides very little information to support a meaningful interpretation of the word. The reader may lack conceptual knowledge about the stalks of fungi, which limits her ability to construct a meaningful sentence. If the reader has never encountered the word before, she may lack syntactical knowledge about how the word should be used. Proficient adult readers know a great deal about vocabulary and syntax, yet they may find the task of generating a meaningful sentence with words such as *pedunculate* very difficult. Children and less proficient adult readers often lack background knowledge of words, concepts, and syntax, which means that the task of generating meaningful sentences with unknown words is nearly impossible.

Memorize the Definition

Another common instructional activity is providing definitions of target words and asking children to memorize them. Nagy (1985, 1988) found that definitional approaches did not generalize well and had no effect on reading comprehension. In other words, children could be taught to memorize word definitions successfully but were not able to comprehend the new words in texts, nor could they use the words generatively in their own writing. Nagy concluded that definitional approaches were not an effective means of increasing vocabulary or comprehension.

Complete Word Searches and Scrambles

When teachers realize that traditional instructional methods are not working, they may turn to teacher supply stores for an alternative approach. They will find a multitude of "vocabulary" workbooks full of worksheets that purport to provide vocabulary instruction. Activities such as word searches and word scrambles have little instructional value for teaching vocabulary. Word searches consist of a matrix of seemingly random letters hiding a number of target words. Children are required to locate and circle the words, which may be listed horizontally, vertically, diagonally, or backwards. In word scrambles, children must unscramble the mixed-up letters, identifying the target words. While word searches and word scrambles may be fun, they are time-consuming, provide no exposure to words in context, and contribute little to children's vocabulary growth. Given the limited time available to teach vocabulary and the vast number of words children need to learn, these activities are difficult to justify.

Nick's Words

Traditional vocabulary instruction often fails to provide children with in-depth word knowledge, as one teacher discovered. Mrs. Simon, the resource teacher, welcomed third grader Nick to her classroom. She watched as he diligently completed the vocabulary worksheets that accompanied his reading book. Nick looked up words in the glossary and copied the definitions. He completed sentences, inserting the appropriate words from the word bank, and filled in the boxes in the publisher-created crossword puzzle. He smiled at her, proud that he could complete the assignment with ease.

Mrs. Simon visited Nick's class later that day during social studies time. The students had completed reading the assigned text and were answering questions on the board. Nick caught sight of Mrs. Simon and asked her for help. He explained that he could not do the assignment because he did not understand the words. As she scanned the textbook, she noticed that three of the words that Nick said he did not know were part of the vocabulary assignment that he had completed in the resource room earlier in the day. She pointed to the textbook. "Nick, look here! I saw you working on these words this morning."

"Really?" Nick replied, looking baffled. "This morning we did vocabulary work from our reading books. This is social studies."

Nick's inability to transfer the definition of language arts words to the comprehension of social studies texts is not surprising. Research has shown that definitional approaches to vocabulary instruction merely increase children's ability to define words but have no effect on reading comprehension (Baumann et al., 2003). Nick needed more effective vocabulary instruction in order to understand his social studies textbook. Instruction that is powerful enough to improve reading comprehension requires a combination of methods that is called *comprehensive vocabulary development* in this book.

COMPREHENSIVE VOCABULARY DEVELOPMENT

Comprehensive vocabulary development is a multifaceted, research-based approach to vocabulary instruction. The model in Figure 1.2 provides an overview of comprehensive vocabulary development, demonstrating how instructional

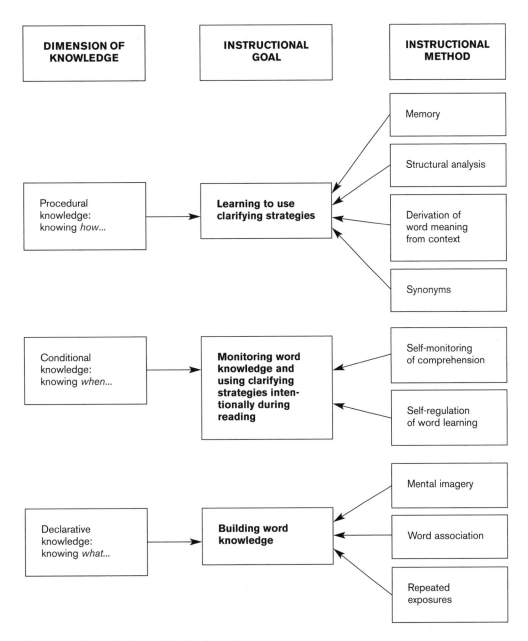

Figure 1.2. Comprehensive vocabulary development.

methods are used to meet instructional goals for three important dimensions of knowledge.

Dimensions of Knowledge

Comprehensive vocabulary development addresses three dimensions of instruction that are essential to vocabulary growth (Ruddell, 1994):

- *Procedural knowledge*—knowing *how* to use vocabulary acquisition strategies intentionally during reading

- *Conditional knowledge*—knowing *when* to use strategies to regulate word learning
- *Declarative word knowledge*—knowing *what* (the words) one needs to know

The comprehensive vocabulary development model provides a conceptual framework for organizing instruction.

Instructional Goals

The following goals drive instruction in each dimension of vocabulary knowledge:

- Children will learn to use effective clarifying strategies (procedural dimension)
- Children will learn to monitor word knowledge and use clarifying strategies intentionally during reading (conditional dimension)
- Children will build in-depth knowledge of important vocabulary words (declarative dimension)

Instructional Methods

Instructional methods are the procedures that are used to attain instructional goals in each dimension of knowledge. For example, mental imagery, word association, and repeated exposures are methods of building word knowledge, the declarative dimension of instruction.

THE TOOLS OF SUCCESS

The Tools of Success are instructional activities, the nuts and bolts of a comprehensive vocabulary development program. These activities are designed to build vocabulary and word-learning skills in each dimension of knowledge. The chart on the facing page explains where in this book each tool can be found. Teachers can use the Tools of Success to plan comprehensive vocabulary instruction to develop the skills and knowledge that the children need in order to read proficiently.

The Tools of Success are presented in Chapters 2–8. (Instruction designed for young children, English language learners, and whole-school implementation are provided in Chapters 9–11, respectively.) Detailed instructions, practice worksheets, and classroom dialogues are provided for the instructional tools. Appendix A contains a glossary of key terms. An answer key for the worksheets appears in Appendix B. Once you have finished reading the book, you can return to the Tools of Success and use them to plan comprehensive vocabulary development instruction.

COMPREHENSIVE VOCABULARY DEVELOPMENT PROGRAM

Dimension	Word-learning skill	Tools of Success	Chapter	Page(s)
Procedural knowledge: Knowing *how*...	Use **CLARIFYING STRATEGIES** to make sense of unfamiliar words encountered during reading.	**Clarifying Strategies Overview**	Chapter 2	19–20
		Clarifying Cue Card	Chapter 2	38
		Clarifying Cue Card for Kids	Chapter 9	138–140, 143
		Clarifying Cue Card with Catch a Cognate (in English and in Spanish)	Chapter 10	149, 156, 157
		Mine Your Memory	Chapter 2	20–21
		Study the Structure	Chapter 2	21–29
		All in the Family	Chapter 2	22, 39
		Prefix Chart	Chapter 2	23, 40
		Attitude Adjustment	Chapter 2	24, 42
		Root Webs	Chapter 2	24–26
		Latin and Greek Root Lists	Chapter 2	26–27, 43–44
		Word Tree	Chapter 2	27–28, 45–46
		Be a Root Detective	Chapter 2	28, 47
		Study the Structure Cue Card (in English)	Chapter 2	28–29, 48
		Study the Structure Cue Card (in Spanish)	Chapter 10	158
		Consider the Context	Chapter 2	29–35
		Be a Context Detective	Chapter 2	30, 49
		Be a Super Sleuth	Chapter 2	30, 50–51
		High-Frequency Signal Words	Chapter 2	31
		Sequence Signal Words	Chapter 2	31–32, 52
		Compare-and-Contrast Signal Words	Chapter 2	32, 53
		Signal-Words Cloze	Chapter 2	32, 54
		Cause-and-Effect Signal Words	Chapter 2	32–33, 55
		Stop for Signal Words	Chapter 2	33, 56–57
		Consider the Context Cue Card (in English)	Chapter 2	58
		Consider the Context Cue Card (in Spanish)	Chapter 10	159
		Substitute a Synonym	Chapter 2	35–36
		Five Steps	Chapter 2	36, 59–60
		Additional Clarifying Strategies	Chapter 2	37
		Ask an Expert	Chapter 2	37
		Place a Post-It	Chapter 2	37
		Catch a Cognate Cue Card (in English and in Spanish)	Chapter 10	149–152, 160, 161
		Catch a Cognate Worksheet	Chapter 10	149–151, 162
Conditional knowledge: Knowing *when*...	Determine levels of word learning. Use comprehension-monitoring devices and other **METACOGNITIVE SKILLS.**	Stop Sign	Chapter 4	73–76
		Zone of Understanding	Chapter 5	78–79
		Stoplight Vocabulary	Chapter 5	79–84, 85–87
		Clarifying Strategy Decision Tree	Chapter 6	92–93, 94
Declarative word knowledge: Knowing *what*...	Acquire in-depth **WORD KNOWLEDGE.** Apply word knowledge to reading comprehension.	Word Study Journal	Chapter 7	103–105, 110–111
		Mental Imagery	Chapter 7	105–106
		Expressive Vocabulary Cloze	Chapter 7	106–107, 112
		Getting Into Words with Poetry	Chapter 7	107–108
		Semantic Maps	Chapter 8	113–114
		Feature Analysis Charts	Chapter 8	114–116, 125, 126
		Word Scales	Chapter 8	116, 127
		More Word Scales	Chapter 8	116, 128
		Picture Prediction	Chapter 8	117–119, 129
		Picture Prediction Response Chart	Chapter 8	119–122, 130
		Title Prediction and Sorting	Chapter 8	122–124

There is no rigidly defined order for teaching children the Tools of Success; however, the clarifying strategies are often taught first because they provide a good foundation for comprehensive vocabulary development. With carefully designed instruction, children internalize the clarifying strategies and are able to infer word meaning from the books that they read. The next step is for students to learn the metacognitive skills that they need to monitor comprehension and regulate clarifying strategy use. Explicit vocabulary instruction is also incorporated and is taught across the curriculum. A variety of declarative tools are used to ensure that children acquire in-depth knowledge of high-utility words. Teachers select the tools they need for each lesson to maximize children's word learning and reading comprehension proficiency.

The following vignette demonstrates how Mr. Thomas used the Tools of Success to help his students read and comprehend a demanding text.

The Tools of Success in Action

Mr. Thomas was planning a reading lesson for his fifth-grade students based on the story *The Life of a Cowboy*. He knew that the story contained a number of challenging words that might limit the children's comprehension. He decided to focus on vocabulary instruction, using the Tools of Success. Mr. Thomas was not sure which words would be difficult for the children, so he selected a conditional tool, Stop Sign, to help them evaluate their word knowledge. Mr. Thomas gave each child a small paper stop sign on a Popsicle stick and asked the children to raise their signs whenever they heard an unknown word. He read the first 2 pages of the story aloud to the children and noted raised stop signs. Mr. Thomas carefully reviewed these words and chose the tools he needed for vocabulary instruction.

Mr. Thomas decided that the word *emergencies* was central to the meaning of the text and had to be explicitly taught to the children. He selected a declarative tool, Semantic Maps, to ensure that the children would acquire in-depth knowledge of this essential word. He wrote the word *emergencies* on the board and helped the children construct a map of words related by meaning. Mr. Thomas also noted that the children had difficulty understanding a number of compound and hyphenated words *(e.g., overturn, panic-stricken, sure-footed, counteract)*. He decided to teach the children how to use a procedural tool (a word-learning strategy), Study the Structure. He carefully modeled the strategy, taking extra time to demonstrate how structural analysis helped him make sense of challenging words in the text.

Once he had completed the vocabulary instruction, Mr. Thomas released responsibility to the students, asking them to finish reading the story independently. Mr. Thomas was pleased to see that children were actively engaged in reading the story and demonstrated strong comprehension of the text. He used the Tools of Success effectively to strengthen the children's vocabulary and to ensure a successful reading experience.

Part II

Teaching
Clarifying Strategies

Chapter 2

Strategies that Strengthen Comprehension

Mrs. Stein sipped her coffee and opened the morning newspaper. Soon she was deeply engrossed in an article about education. Finishing the first part of the article on the front page, she flipped through the newspaper to the second half of the article on page 6. She was annoyed to find that a large inkblot down the center of the page obscured one or more words in each line of the text. Mrs. Stein was very interested in the article, so she persevered, using context clues to infer the identity of the missing words. Although this reading experience entailed a great deal of extra effort, Mrs. Stein was able to read and comprehend the article.

Good readers know what to do when they encounter missing or unfamiliar words. They use strategies, or problem-solving methods, to infer text meaning. But most children do not know how to solve word-learning problems and must be provided with explicit strategy instruction. This chapter provides methods for teaching children the clarifying strategies that good readers implement intuitively to improve word learning and reading comprehension.

When you give a man a fish, he eats for one day. When you teach him to fish, he eats for a lifetime. Everyone has heard that Chinese proverb and understands the message. It is more important to teach people skills that will allow them to help themselves than to give them aid that makes them dependent on the donor. Most vocabulary instruction entails *giving* children "fish," that is, words that the teacher selects and explicitly teaches. While some explicit instruction is necessary, this method increases children's dependence on the teacher. Children must be taught independent word-learning strategies that *teach* them to fish, that is, to acquire new vocabulary for a lifetime.

Once teachers decide to do the latter, they are confronted with important questions: Which strategies are most effective in enhancing comprehension? How do teachers explain these powerful tools to children and help children learn to implement the strategies independently during reading? Instruction begins with the Clarifying Cue Card (Lubliner, 2001; see p. 38).

The Clarifying Cue Card comprises four strategies (Mine Your Memory, Study the Structure, Consider the Context, and Substitute a Synonym) that closely mirror the strategic behavior of good readers. Each strategy works differently, and no

strategy is always effective. Additional tools (Ask an Expert and Place a Post-It) are provided for use when the clarifying strategies do not work. The goal of Clarifying Cue Card instruction is to help children learn to "fish in all kinds of water," manipulating strategies flexibly and internalizing effective word-learning skills.

The Clarifying Cue Card was designed as a temporary scaffold to be used during the early stages of strategy instruction. Teachers do not simply give the cue card to children and tell them to use it. They must provide a great deal of explicit instruction and practice with each word-learning strategy. This helps children gain control over the strategies, increasing the likelihood that they will be able to use them during independent reading. Once children internalize the strategies, they discard the cue card, a scaffold that is no longer necessary. Chapters 9 and 10 describe the use of the Clarifying Cue Card with younger children and with English language learners, respectively.

MINE YOUR MEMORY

Clarifying strategy instruction begins with Mine Your Memory, which children usually learn readily and implement effectively. The rationale for incorporating this strategy into word-learning instruction is grounded in research. Children construct word meaning gradually through repeated exposures as they encounter words during reading. In fact, vocabulary experts estimate that up to 10 exposures to a word are required for in-depth vocabulary learning to occur (Nagy, 1985, 1988; Nagy & Herman 1984). Children encounter new words continually and acquire an initial hazy understanding of word meaning that becomes more precise with every encounter. During any given time period, children may be learning up to 1,600 words (Carey, 1978). Children can be taught to access these partially learned words in memory, thereby expanding their vocabulary and helping them to infer the meaning of texts. Without strategy instruction, children tend to skip words that look unfamiliar. Once they learn the strategy Mine Your Memory, they become quite skilled at recalling previous encounters with words. Most children report that this is the easiest and most effective word-learning strategy that they are taught.

Mine Your Memory instruction is based on a high-interest book filled with rich vocabulary. When the teacher reads the book aloud to the children, she pauses when she encounters a challenging word. She thinks aloud as she ponders the meaning of the word, identifying previous encounters with the word that help to clarify word meaning. The teacher continues reading until encountering another difficult word, pauses, and invites the children to reflect on the word. "Have you ever heard that word before?" she asks. The teacher engages the children in a discussion of prior encounters with the word. She points out to the children that the

Mine Your Memory strategy helps them learn words and construct meaning from a text.

Mr. Dean's Class

Mr. Dean's fourth graders had just come in from recess. They bounded into the room and quickly settled down as he passed out a children's news magazine. Mr. Dean asked the children to follow along as he read from an article about South Africa: "The southern tip of Africa is a medley of cultures and landscapes"(Time Inc., 2002, p. 2).

Mr. Dean stopped reading. "Wow, these are hard words!" he said, eyeing the children. "Does anyone know what a medley is?" The children sat quietly, pondering the question. Courtney raised her hand.

"In Girl Scouts we sing a lot of medleys. They're songs put together into one big song."

Mr. Dean smiled, delighted with the response. "Great job clarifying the word *medley*, Courtney! How did you figure it out? Did you use any of the clarifying strategies?"

Courtney explained, "Well, I knew right away that the word was familiar. But I wasn't sure what it meant in the article. When I mined my memory I remembered the Girl Scouts songs and then I knew what it meant."

Mr. Dean asked the children, "How many of you remember singing medleys?" (Most of the children raised their hands.) "So, most of you already knew this word, but you did not realize it. That's the point of Mine Your Memory. You dig into your memory and pull out those words you already know. This is a really powerful strategy that will help you understand a lot of hard words." Mr. Dean reminded the students that they had already learned about the meaning of the word *culture*. He asked another student, Ari, what a medley of cultures could be.

"Is it different groups of people put together, like a medley of songs?" Ari asked hesitantly.

"Exactly!" Mr. Dean praised Ari's response and returned to the magazine. Although this was a current events lesson, he embedded clarifying strategies for word learning into his instruction. This helps the children learn to apply such strategies flexibly to a range of texts.

STUDY THE STRUCTURE

Mr. Dean's Class

Mr. Dean continued to read the article about South Africa with his fourth-grade students. He stopped after reading the following line in the magazine: "With its dramatic mountains..." (Time Inc., 2002, p. 2).

"Okay, we better stop here! What are dramatic mountains?" Mr. Dean asked, emphasizing the word *dramatic*.

Leora, who loved theater, eagerly answered, "I know! It's like drama."

Mr. Dean looked puzzled. "How can mountains be like drama?" he asked.

Leora explained, "Drama is a story that makes you feel like you're in another world. It's amazing! So, I think dramatic mountains are amazing too. They're so high or beautiful, when you see them, it's like you're in another world."

Mr. Dean gave a thumbs-up to Leora. "That's a perfect clarification of the phrase *dramatic mountains*. Which strategy did Leora use?"

Nicole raised her hand. "She used Study the Structure because *drama* was inside the word."

Mr. Dean nodded approvingly and moved on with the lesson.

Study the Structure is a particularly complex clarifying strategy for children to learn. It entails learning word parts and applying the knowledge strategically to infer word meaning. Teachers begin instruction with base words, then move on to affixes (prefixes and suffixes, including inflected suffixes such as *-s, -ed,* and *-ing*), followed by high-frequency Latin and Greek roots. Initial instruction focuses on helping children recognize words that are part of the same word family. For example, *build* is a base word that is part of a word family that includes *building, builds, rebuild,* and many other words. If children learn to use structural clues with base words and common prefixes and suffixes, they can infer the meanings of up to 80% of words containing affixes (White, Power, & White, 1989). (For further discussion of base words, high-frequency Latin and Greek roots and affixes, and structural analysis, see Henry, 2003.)

All in the Family

The universal concept of family relationships is used as a basis of instruction in the activity All in the Family (see p. 39). Children readily grasp the idea that words are related to each other just as the children are related the members of their own families. All in the Family helps children recognize and construct meaning for related words encountered during reading.

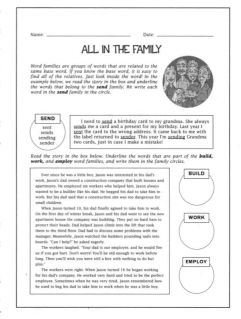

Affixes

A vast number of affixes and roots are found in the books children read. To make the most of limited instructional time, teachers focus instruction on the word parts that children will encounter most frequently. For example, a small number of negative prefixes (i.e., *un-, in-, im-, il-,* and *ir-*) account for 37% of words with prefixes that children are likely to encounter (White, Sowell, & Yanagihara, 1989).

Mrs. Yoshi's Class

Mrs. Yoshi, a sixth-grade teacher, decided to spend part of her language arts block on vocabulary instruction. Noting that her struggling readers often failed to recognize words containing affixes even when knowing the base words, Mrs. Yoshi devoted several lessons to this topic. She began by introducing her students to high-frequency negative prefixes, using a prefix chart (see p. 40). She placed a transparency of the chart on the overhead projector and showed the children how to record the word *unnecessary*. Mrs. Yoshi modeled filling in the chart, writing the word, the prefix *(un-)*, the prefix's meaning *(not)*, the base word *(necessary)*, the base word's meaning *(something you need)*, and the meaning of the word created by adding the prefix to the base word *(something you don't need)*. Mrs. Yoshi selected another word beginning with the prefix un- *(unusual)* and asked the children to help fill in the chart. Then she asked the children generate a list of additional examples.

"Who can think of another word that starts with *un-?*" Mrs. Yoshi asked. The children came up with a number of words, including *unlikely, unforgettable, unfair,* and *unlucky,* which Mrs. Yoshi listed on the board. She passed out copies of the prefix chart and asked the children to select words from the list and to fill in their prefix charts. When the children completed the task, Mrs. Yoshi called the class together and invited the children to take turns filling in the chart on the overhead transparency.

When they had finished filling in the chart, Mrs. Yoshi announced, "I have a challenge for you! Do you think you can use a word with and without a prefix in the same sentence?" The children thought for a few minutes and then began to raise their hands.

Mike came up with a sentence that made the other children laugh. "I think it's unfair when we get homework over the weekend, but it's fair if we have enough time to get it done before Friday."

Mrs. Yoshi jokingly replied, "Kind teachers give their students plenty of warning before being unkind enough to assign homework over the weekend." The students laughed at the clever exchange. More important, they gained insight as to how prefixes can be used to alter word meaning.

During the next few days Mrs. Yoshi used the prefix chart (see p. 40) and word lists (see p. 41) to introduce the children to additional words with prefixes. Mrs. Yoshi also

---

Name: _____ Date: _____

PREFIX CHART

Prefixed word	Prefix	Prefix's meaning	Base word (word without prefix)	Base word's meaning	Prefixed word's meaning

---

WORDS WITH NEGATIVE PREFIXES

Level 4

dis-	il-, in-	mis-	un-	
disagree	illegal	misbehave	unattached	unlikely
disappear	incomplete	misfortune	unattractive	unlucky
disapprove	incorrect	misjudge	uncertain	unnecessary
discomfort	independence	misplace	unchanged	unpleasant
disconnect	insane	mistreat	unclean	unprepared
discover	invisible	misunderstand	undisturbed	unprotected
dislike			unexpected	unready
disobey			unexplored	unreasonable
displease			unfair	unsafe
			unfinished	unseen
			unfriendly	unskilled
			unhappy	untrue
			unharmed	unwanted
			unheard of	unwelcome
			unimportant	unwilling
			uninteresting	unwise
			unkind	unworthy
			unknown	unwritten

Level 6

dis-	il-, in-	mis-	un-	
discontented	inability	misfit	unable	unlike
displace	inaccurate	misinformation	unaware	unlock
dissimilar	incapable	mislead	unbearable	unorganized
	inconsiderate	mismanage	uncivilized	unsteady
	incredible	mispronounce	unconquered	unsuccessful
	incurable	mistrust	unconscious	untidy
	indescribable		uncover	unusual
	ineffective		uneasy	unwanted
	inexact		unfortunate	unwise
	inexperienced		unidentified	unworthy
	innumerable		uninjured	

paused to point out words with prefixes in the children's textbooks and encouraged them to watch for words containing prefixes as they read independently. She was pleased to see that the children's comprehension of words containing prefixes grew steadily over the next few weeks.

The lists of words with prefixes shown on page 41 are based on information found in *The Living Word Vocabulary* (Dale & O'Rourke, 1981), which lists commonly used words and identifies the percentage of children who know the words at particular grade levels (at the fourth, sixth, eighth, tenth, and twelfth grades and at the postsecondary level). Page 41 shows fourth- and sixth-grade lists of words with prefixes (known by two thirds of children at these levels, respectively).

Attitude Adjustment (High-Frequency Negative Prefixes)

Once children have been introduced to high-frequency prefixes they need additional practice manipulating word parts. The instructional activity Attitude Adjustment (see p. 42) addresses the manipulation of high-frequency negative prefixes.

Attitude Adjustment uses a comical letter to teach children to recognize and understand high-frequency negative prefixes (*un-*, *in-*, *im-*, *il-*). The purpose of the activity is to help children gain control over these prefixes, increasing their ability to use the Study the Structure strategy effectively. After the teacher has read the letter aloud, the children work together, deleting the negative prefixes and rereading the text. (Not all negative prefixes appear in Attitude Adjustment.)

Children enjoy the humorous aspects of Attitude Adjustment and are eager to write their own "bad attitude" letters, using the lists of words with negative prefixes (see p. 41) as sources of additional vocabulary. Grouping prefixes with similar meaning and extending instruction to include writing activities help children acquire in-depth knowledge of prefix meaning. This type of instruction promotes lexical access so that children can clarify words containing affixes readily.

Root Webs

In the Root Webs activity, the teacher begins Latin and Greek root word instruction by introducing a high-frequency root such as *form*. She writes the root on the board, defines it, and asks the children to brainstorm words from the same word family. The teacher records all of the words that the children generate on the board. She asks the children to identify the words on the list that have prefixes and underline the prefixes. The teacher asks the children to select words on the list that do not have inflected endings (e.g., *-ed, -s, -es, -ing*) or suffixes for the first level of the root web. She circles the words that the children suggest and writes these words on the root web and links them to the root (see Figure 2.1).

The teacher discusses each word in the web, explaining how prefixes and roots combine to create word meaning. Then the teacher points out words on the list that have inflected endings and other suffixes. She adds words with the inflected ending *-ed* to the root web and invites children to add additional inflected endings (e.g., the verb endings *-s, -ing*). With the children's contributions, the root web now looks like Figure 2.2.

Finally, the teacher introduces the suffix *-er* and models adding it to the word *inform*. She invites the children to add words, pausing to explain that suffixes do not work in every combination of prefixes and roots. The teacher points to the word *information* on the word list the children generated, suggesting that they add words ending in *-ation* or *-tion* to the root web. Now the root web (see Figure 2.3) contains 24 words based on the root *form*. The teacher points out to the children

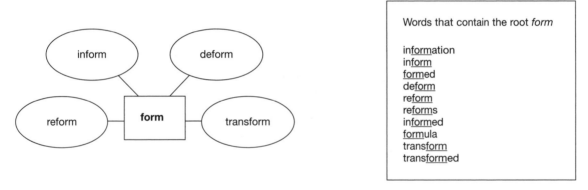

Figure 2.1. Root web 1, with a list of *form* words children have suggested. This initial web shows the root and prefixed words that the children have suggested (without inflected suffixes).

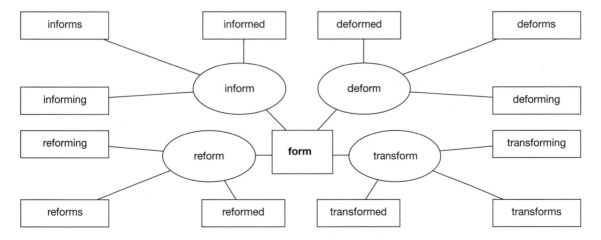

Figure 2.2. Root web 2. This intermediate web adds words with inflected endings for verbs, *-ed, -s,* and *-ing.*

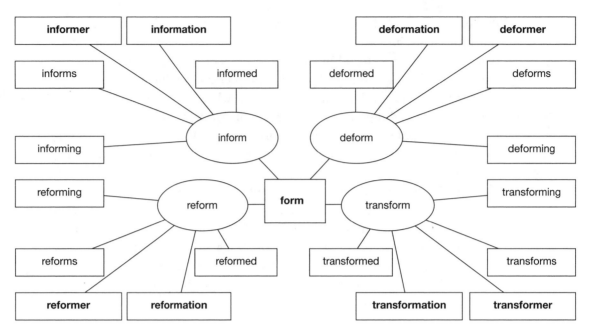

Figure 2.3.   Root web 3. This final web adds words with the inflected endings *-er* and *-ation.*

that knowing how to use roots, prefixes, and suffixes to construct meaning provides the children with powerful word-learning skills.

Now that the teacher has modeled the process of creating root webs, she is ready to transfer responsibility to the students. She passes out copies of Latin and Greek root lists (see pp. 43–44) and asks the children to select roots to web. Then children work in pairs constructing their own root webs that they share with the class.

Latin and Greek Root Lists

Once children have learned the high-fre-quency affixes and have worked with root webs, they are ready for instruction in important Latin and Greek roots. Pages 43 and 44 include Latin and Greek root lists, respectively, that can be used for a variety of instructional activities. These particular roots were selected based on a word-fre-quency guide for children's texts (Zeno, Ivens, Millard, & Duvvuri, 1995). The word-frequency guide lists all of the words found in school literature (novels and text-books) and the number of times each word appears at various grade levels. I examined roots found in books such as *Word Journeys*

LATIN ROOT LIST

ROOT	WHAT IT MEANS	EXAMPLE
dict	to say	contradict (say something against)
equ	the same	equal (having the same value or qual-ity)
fac/fact/fect	to do, to make	factory (a place where things are made)
form	shape	deformed (misshapen)
ject	throw	eject (to throw out)
jud/jur/jus	judge	prejudice (negative judgment about people)
loc	place	location (a place)
man	hand	manual (by hand)
mem	remember	memorize (learn something by heart)
port	to carry	transport (to carry from place to place)
prim/prin	first	primary (first or most important)
ques/quer	to ask	question (something you ask)
scrib/script	to write	manuscript (a written draft of a book)
sens/sent	to feel	sensation (a feeling)
spec/spect	to look	inspect (look at very carefully)
struct	build	structure (something that has been built)
tract	drag or pull	extract (to pull out of something)
trans	across	transfer (move something from one place to another)
val	to be strong/worth	valuable (to be worth a lot)
voc	voice, to call	advocate (to voice support; a person who does so)

(Ganske, 2000) and *English Words from Latin and Greek Elements* (Ayers, 1986) and identified a large number of high-frequency Latin roots. Only those Latin roots that were linked to at least 100 derived words (words taken from a source) at the sixth-grade level were included in the Latin Root List (see p. 43). The frequency of words derived from Greek roots was much lower, so Greek roots with at least 25 derived words at the sixth-grade level were included in the Greek Root List (see p. 44).

When children learn high-frequency roots, they gain understanding of the words that appear frequently in the elementary curriculum and acquire the tools to make sense of more challenging words. For exam-

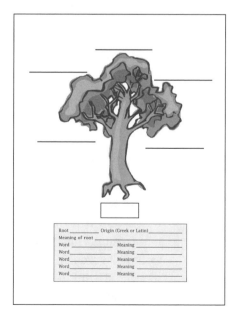

ple, the high-frequency Latin root *port* means *to carry from one place to another.* Once children learn this root they are capable of understanding words such as *transport* (appears 31 times in school texts, according to Zeno et al., 1995), *export* (appears 3 times), *portable* (appears 2 times, according to Zeno et al.), and so forth. In addition, children can make sense of such words as *deportation* that do not appear in school texts until the postsecondary level.

Word Tree

The Word Tree activity provides children with additional practice and flexibility in manipulating high-frequency Latin and Greek roots and affixes. The teacher begins by preparing a Word Tree transparency (see p. 45) and hands out copies of the Word Tree worksheet (see p. 46). He models filling in the first root, *spect,* and discusses the meaning of each derived word that the children identify. He explains how affixes are combined with roots to determine word meaning. The teacher models selecting the next root from the Latin or Greek root list (see pp. 43 and 44, respectively). Then he asks each child to work with a partner to complete the rest of the word trees on the worksheet. When the children finish the activity, they share their word trees with the class, discussing the meanings of the words that are derived from the roots. To increase the likelihood that children will internalize the meaning of Latin and Greek roots and their derived words, the teacher displays the children's Word Tree worksheets on the bulletin board.

Be a Root Detective

Vocabulary interventions often succeed in increasing children's vocabulary knowledge or strategic skills without improving children's reading comprehension. Apparently, these interventions fail to provide children with knowledge and skills that they can transfer beyond the original instructional setting. To increase reading proficiency, children must learn to transfer their knowledge of words and word parts to the strategic comprehension of texts. Instruction begins with a specially designed text. Natural texts do not usually provide sufficient opportunities for children to practice inferring word meaning from structure. The text for the Be a Root Detective activity (see p. 47), based on fifth-grade social studies and science vocabulary, was specially constructed to provide Study the Structure strategy practice.

The Be a Root Detective text includes 10 words (*inspecting, artifact, photograph, location, extract, technique, microscopic, description, dictated,* and *monograph*) found on the Latin and Greek root lists (see pp. 43–44). Proficient students can be challenged to find additional words derived from Latin and Greek roots, such as *logical* and *chronological*.

Study the Structure Cue Card

Children gain increasing flexibility as they practice implementing Study the Structure with specially designed texts such as the one in the Be a Root Detective activity. Now it is time to move students on to using regular textbooks and novels. It is very important to help the children transfer their emerging strategy skills to clarifying words in authentic texts. The Study the Structure Cue Card (see p. 48) reminds children to use structure clues while reading and instructs children to take a mental "snapshot" after they have analyzed an unknown word so that they can remember its parts later. The intent is to ensure that children fully internalize this clarifying strategy and use it spontaneously during independent reading. Chapter 10 contains a Spanish translation of the Study the Structure Cue Card (see p. 158).

CONSIDER THE CONTEXT

How useful is context? Many vocabulary experts assert that it is a major source of vocabulary growth and reading comprehension (Nagy et al., 1986, 1987). Others argue that context is tricky and does not often provide helpful clues to word meaning (Beck et al., 2002). According to research, context is more likely to help a child infer word meaning under the following conditions: 1) The text provides plenty of information that supports inference, 2) the target word and the contextual support are closely linked, 3) the child has partial word knowledge, and 4) the child has background knowledge related to the unknown word (Nagy et al., 1986, 1987).

Context is an important strategy that helps children "learn to fish." Explicit Consider the Context strategy lessons followed by opportunities to practice are essential components of instruction. Teachers also increase strategy learning by modeling Consider the Context whenever appropriate teachable moments occur.

STUDY THE STRUCTURE CUE CARD

When you find a word you don't understand, try this strategy:

STUDY THE STRUCTURE
Try to use the word's structure (how it is made) to help you. Do you know the mystery word's root? Does it have a prefix or suffix that you know? Try to use clues in the word to figure out the meaning.

Base words
Base words are building blocks that are used to make many other words. When you find a mystery word, look for the base word and see if it helps you figure out the meaning.

Roots
Many words in English have Greek or Latin roots. The root can help you figure out the meaning of the mystery word. Check your Greek and Latin root lists to find out.

Prefixes
A prefix is a beginning part that helps give a word meaning. Does the mystery word have a prefix that you know?

Suffixes
A suffix is an ending part that helps give a word meaning. Does the mystery word have a suffix that you know?

SNAPSHOT
Pretend you have a camera, and take a picture of the word and the sentence it is in so that you will remember the word the next time you see it. Each time you see the mystery word, it will be easier to remember.

Mr. Dean's Class

Mr. Dean was reading from an article about soccer in South Africa to his fourth-grade students: "The entire country rejoiced when the national team Bafana Bafana, won the African National Cup in 1996" (Time Inc., 2002, p. 2).

Mr. Dean stopped and asked the students what the word *rejoiced* means. Almost every hand in the room waved eagerly. Mr. Dean called on Lenny, who replied, "They were happy."

Mr. Dean asked Lenny which strategy he used to clarify the word.

"Well, I kind of knew the word already, so first I mined my memory. I remembered that we read this story about people rejoicing when their sons came home from war. But I also used Consider the Context. You can tell the people were happy because it says their team won."

Ari added, "You can also tell what the word means because *rejoiced* sounds like *joy* and that means the same thing as *happy*."

Mr. Dean replied, "That's right! You each used a different clarifying strategy to make sense of the word *rejoiced*. In this case, all of the strategies worked."

Mr. Dean's fourth-grade lesson used an authentic text that facilitates the children's use of Consider the Context. The article provides rich contextual support that is close to the target word *rejoiced*. The children had partial word knowledge that makes using context easier. Many of them are soccer players, so their interest was heightened and they had plenty of background knowledge to apply to word comprehension.

The instructional implications of this example are considerable. Background knowledge facilitates the use of context, so if children are not familiar with concepts presented in the text, they need instruction prior to reading. Background knowledge can be activated with pictures, films, and word-prediction activities (see Chapter 8). The purpose of this preteaching is to ensure that unfamiliar words in the text are new labels for known vocabulary, rather than entirely new concepts for the children. Learning new labels for unfamiliar concepts is a much more difficult task for children and can be avoided with appropriate instruction.

Be a Context Detective

Proficient readers know that context does not always work, but most children lack the ability to think critically about strategy effectiveness. Teachers build flexible strategic thinking by providing examples of context that is helpful, not helpful, and misleading. Children also tend to give up quickly if they do not find context clues very close to the target word. Teachers help children develop flexible strategic skills by teaching them to hunt for context clues throughout the text. The terms *next door, in the neighborhood,* and *far away* are used to characterize the proximity of contextual support for the unfamiliar word. The Be a Context Detective instructional worksheet

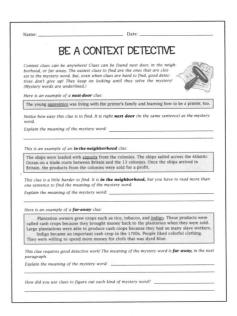

(see p. 49), designed for the upper-elementary grades and beyond, reinforces children's understanding of context clues. (Similar activities for students in primary grades are included in Chapter 9.)

Be a Super Sleuth

Children need practice using new word-learning tools to transfer their skills to texts. The Be a Super Sleuth activity (see pp. 50–51) provides children with the opportunity to practice identifying and using different kinds of context clues. The purpose of Be a Super Sleuth is to help children infer word meaning from texts that include comma clues (appositives), explanation clues, feeling clues, or opposition clues.

High-Frequency Signal Words

Students often struggle to make sense of content-area textbooks even when they understand the key vocabulary. One factor that contributes to textbook difficulty is the frequent use of *signal words*. Signal words are usually adverbs that indicate a particular kind of relationship between concepts in a text. Students often fail to notice signal words and thus miss essential clues about the meaning of text passages. Explicit instruction and guided practice in using signal words increases children's comprehension of content-area textbooks substantially. Table 2.1 contains high-frequency signal words grouped into categories based on meaning.

Sequence Signal Words

Teachers begin instruction by pointing out signal words as they read aloud simple nonfiction books to children. Children quickly learn to recognize signal words such as those that indicate sequence in the life cycles of various animals. Teachers can use a sequence chart and create simple cloze (fill-in-the-blank) activities to reinforce signal-word instruction. In the initial stages of instruction, the teacher and children complete the cloze activity together, discussing possible word choices for each blank. The

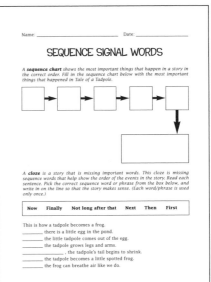

Table 2.1.   High-frequency signal words

Definition words	Example words	Addition words	Sequence words	Comparison words	Opposition words	Cause-and-effect words
means	for example	also	first...	similar	in contrast	because
refers to	for instance	another	second...	just like	but	therefore
consists of	such as	furthermore	next	in the same way	yet	so
in other words	including	in addition	then	in comparison	on the other hand	consequently
		moreover	finally	likewise	however	due to
			soon			so that

Sequence Signal Words activity (see p. 52), based on the book *Tale of a Tadpole* (Wallace, 1998), includes a sequence chart and cloze passage. The activity is suitable for a wide range of age groups and helps to build awareness of sequence signal words.

Compare and Contrast Signal Words, and Signal-Words Cloze

Teaching children to recognize signal words is particularly important as they enter the upper-elementary grades. Social studies and science textbooks contain large numbers of signal words that often contribute to comprehension problems. Children need to focus on signal words as context clues as they read content-area texts.

Teachers can increase the effectiveness of signal-word instruction by using graphic organizers to demonstrate the relationship between concepts in the text. The Venn diagram in the Compare and Contrast Signal Words activity (see p. 53) and the Signal-Words Cloze activity (see p. 54) are designed to help children learn and recognize signal words they are likely to encounter in social studies textbooks. Teachers can design similar activities for signal words often found in science and other content-area textbooks.

Cause-and-Effect Signal Words

Learning to identify causes and effects in content-area texts is another important skill in the upper-elementary grades. Teaching children the meaning of cause-and-effect signal words develops their ability to comprehend challenging texts. Teachers can introduce the Cause-and-Effect Signal Words (see p. 55) using the folk tale "The Little Red Hen." The teacher begins instruction by reading aloud the story to the children. She helps the children identify the causes of the problem (the animals' refusal to help) and the effect (the hen's decision not to share the bread). The teacher asks the children to use signal words to fill in the cloze passage at the bottom of the page 55. This activity may appear simplistic but is actually quite com-

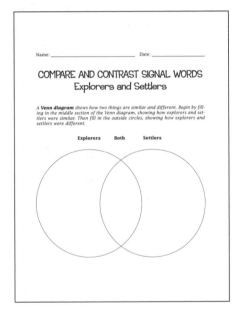

plex. Children must analyze the story, identifying key causes and effects. Then they fill in the blanks in the cloze activity, working with cause-and-effect signal words. This activity can be used with a wide range of age groups and helps to build vocabulary and text analysis skills that children transfer from folk tales to content-area textbooks and novels.

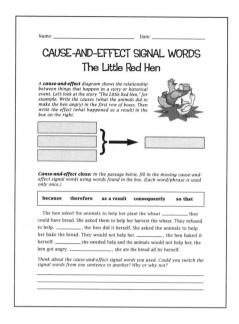

Stop for Signal Words

Upper-grade teachers explicitly teach children to recognize signal words using the Stop for Signal Words activity (see pp. 56–57). Grouping signal words into semantic categories helps children identify and comprehend related words.

Teachers explicitly teach each category of signal words to the children, using the examples provided on pages 56–57 to model the construction of sentences containing signal words. Teachers ask the children to generate their own sentences for each signal word in the category and encourage them to share their sentences with the class. When the children read the social studies textbook, teachers point out examples of signal words and discuss the importance of these words in conveying the meaning of the text. Extending signal-word instruction through the use of cloze activities is discussed later in this chapter.

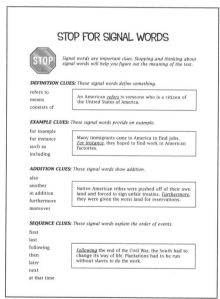

Mrs. Chin's Class

The following discussion in Mrs. Chin's fourth-grade classroom illustrates the Stop for Signal Words activity. Mrs. Chin discussed signal words found in a passage from the social studies textbook.

Mrs. Chin: (Reads the text passage aloud) "The Native Americans received food and shelter in the missions; however, many of them longed to return to their villages."

(Begins discussion) Okay, everyone. Please take out your Stop for Signal Word sheets, the ones with the big stop sign on top. Remember, we went over the different kinds of signal words? (Children nod). Does anyone see a signal word in this sentence?

Maurice: Yeah, it's however.

Mrs. Chin: Good, Maurice! What kind of signal word is it?

Monica: (looks at the Stop for Signal Words sheet) A contrasting one?

Mrs. Chin: That's right. Now, I want you to tell me why this word is so important.

Maurice: Because it tells what the Native Americans wanted to do.

Mrs. Chin: Okay, what did they want to do?

Maurice: They wanted to go back to their homes.

Mrs. Chin: Right! Now, where's the contrasting information?

Maurice: Umm...I don't know...

Mrs. Chin: Maurice has given us a good start by pointing out that *however* is a contrasting word. He also told us that the Native Americans wanted to go back to their villages. Can anyone tell us what the contrasting point is?

Dana: Well, it's contrasting how the missions were good and bad for the people at the same time. Even though the Native Americans got food, they still wanted to go home to their villages.

Mrs. Chin: Exactly! Dana, you explained that very well, and you used another signal word that means the same thing. *Even though* and *however* are both contrasting words. Whenever you see contrasting signal words, you want to look for things that are not the same.

Mrs. Chin needs to point out examples of signal words frequently as her fourth graders grapple with the complex language in social studies texts. She should also give the children cloze activities and opportunities to work together to find and explain signal words encountered during reading. This instruction is vitally important in providing the children with the skills to comprehend upper-grade textbooks and literature. Important signal words that children need to learn are included in Table 2.1 on page 31 and in the worksheet on pages 56–57.

More Signal-Word Cloze Passages

The teacher can extend signal-word instruction by constructing cloze passages from children's textbooks or from a reading anthology. The teacher copies a page of text, deletes signal words using correction fluid or correction tape, provides students with copies of this cloze passage, and models filling in the passage. Children can try different words in the same signal-word category to determine whether the words can be used interchangeably. These signal-word activities enhance children's ability to comprehend challenging texts.

The following cloze passage was created from the fifth-grade social studies book *America Will Be* (Armento, Nash, Salter, & Wixson, 1991). The *signal words* (*before, such as, at that time, for example, so, however, thus*) are used to fill in the blanks in this passage about the Industrial Revolution.

_____ 1770, most goods— _____ clothing and shoes—were made by hand. _____ , most Americans lived on farms. A family member might need a shirt, _____ . _____ , someone in the family would spin wool into thread, weave it into cloth, and sew the shirt.

Americans did not make all their own goods, _____ . Some things—such as glass, tools, and some cloth—were made in Britain and imported. During the mid-1700s British inventors looked for ways to make these goods more cheaply and _____ increase their sales. (Armento et al., 1991, p. 422)

Consider the Context Cue Card

Instruction based on the Consider the Context Cue Card (see p. 58) helps children learn to recognize and use different types of context clues. Children are taught to recognize explanation clues that provide information about word meaning and to recognize appositives, definitions enclosed in commas following the target words. Students learn to infer word meaning based on feeling (emotional) clues in the text. Children also learn to interpret tricky oppositional words such as *but, however, although, on the other hand,* and *in spite of* that provide important clues about word meaning. The Consider the Context Cue Card can be used for instruction with children who are in the upper-elementary grades and beyond. Chapter 10 contains a Spanish translation of Consider the Context Cue Card (see p. 159).

SUBSTITUTE A SYNONYM

Substitute a Synonym is a secondary strategy that is used after a word has been clarified with one or more of the primary strategies Mine Your Memory, Study the Structure, and Consider the Context. This secondary strategy helps students to check word meaning to ensure that it makes sense. Teachers increase the effectiveness of this strategy by allowing children to choose a word, a phrase, or an example to check word meaning.

M Dean' s Class

Mr. Dean's fourth graders clarified several words in the current events article they were reading, "Welcome to South Africa" (Time Inc., 2002). After they finished clarifying the word *rejoiced*, Mr. Dean asked the fourth graders to come up with a synonym to check that Lenny's clarification of the word *rejoiced* was correct. Joel raised his hand and suggested the word *celebrated*. Mr. Dean asked him to try the synonym so that the class can decide if it works. Joel read the sentence with the synonym: "The entire country celebrated when the national team Bafana Bafana, won the African National Cup in 1996."

Lenny raised his hand. "I think *was happy* works better. The entire country *was happy* when the national team Bafana Bafana won."

Mr. Dean pointed out that both synonyms work well. "You can use a word, a phrase or an example when you substitute a synonym. The point is to check and make sure that you understand the word. Did Joel and Lenny check the word, and did it make sense?" (The children nodded.) "Good job, boys!" Mr. Dean gave Joel and Lenny a thumbs-up and returned to the text.

Five Steps: Substitute a Synonym

Teachers such as Mr. Dean model the use of clarifying strategies extensively and engage children in text-based discussions. This type of instruction helps children learn to implement clarifying strategies with a wide range of texts. The Five Steps: Substitute a Synonym activity (see pp. 59–60) provides additional practice in using the Substitute a Synonym clarifying strategy to figure out the meaning of challenging words encountered during reading.

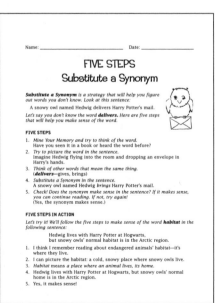

Name: _____   Date: _____

FIVE STEPS
Substitute a Synonym

Substitute a Synonym is a strategy that will help you figure out words you don't know. Look at this sentence:

A snowy owl named Hedwig delivers Harry Potter's mail.

*Let's say you don't know the word **delivers**. Here are five steps that will help you make sense of the word.*

FIVE STEPS
1. *Mine Your Memory and try to think of the word.*
   Have you seen it in a book or heard the word before?
2. *Try to picture the word in the sentence.*
   Imagine Hedwig flying into the room and dropping an envelope in Harry's hands.
3. *Think of other words that mean the same thing.*
   (*delivers*—gives, brings)
4. *Substitute a Synonym in the sentence.*
   A snowy owl named Hedwig *brings* Harry Potter's mail.
5. *Check! Does the synonym make sense in the sentence? If it makes sense, you can continue reading. If not, try again!*
   (Yes, the synonym makes sense.)

FIVE STEPS IN ACTION
*Let's try it! We'll follow the five steps to make sense of the word **habitat** in the following sentence:*

Hedwig lives with Harry Potter at Hogwarts,
but snowy owls' normal habitat is in the Arctic region.

1. I think I remember reading about endangered animals' habitat—it's where they live.
2. I can picture the habitat: a cold, snowy place where snowy owls live.
3. *Habitat* means *a place where an animal lives, its home.*
4. Hedwig lives with Harry Potter at Hogwarts, but snowy owls' normal home is in the Arctic region.
5. Yes, it makes sense!

ADDITIONAL CLARIFYING STRATEGIES

Catch a Cognate, Ask an Expert, and Place a Post-It

Additional clarifying strategies that children may need include the following: Catch a Cognate, Ask an Expert, and Place a Post-It. Catch a Cognate is designed for classes that include Spanish-speaking children. Instructional methods for this strategy are provided in Chapter 10. Ask an Expert is intended for use during cooperative group work. When children are working together, clarifying words as they read, they can ask a peer expert to help them figure out the meaning of unfamiliar words. Place a Post-It is used when all of the other strategies have failed. The Post-It signifies the need to look up the word or discuss it with the teacher after reading time has ended. Ask an Expert and Place a Post-It are less effective strategies than the four main clarifying strategies, but they convey an important point: *Children may not skip words while reading.* Every word must be clarified or marked for later attention. This is a critically important point in fostering children's vocabulary growth. The more often children wrestle with unfamiliar words, the more layers of meaning are constructed, and the greater the likelihood that word learning will occur. Skipping words, on the other hand, provides minimal exposure to new words and lessens engagement with texts. Once children have been taught the word-learning strategies, they are ready to put them all together and use the strategies with texts.

CLARIFYING CUE CARD

When you find a word you don't understand, try the following strategies:

MINE YOUR MEMORY

Have you ever seen this word before? Can you remember what it means?

STUDY THE STRUCTURE

Do you know the root or base word? Does the word have a prefix or suffix that you know? Try to use clues in the word to figure out the meaning.

CONSIDER THE CONTEXT

Look at the information in the sentence and the whole paragraph. Can you figure out the meaning of the word?

SUBSTITUTE A SYNONYM

When you think you know what the word means, try putting a word with a similar meaning in the sentence. Does it make sense?

If the strategies don't work, try these:

ASK AN EXPERT

Does someone in your group know what the word means? Can you figure it out together?

PLACE A POST-IT

If you can't figure out the meaning of the word, put a Post-It by the word, and check with the teacher or look it up in the dictionary later.

From Lubliner, S. (2001). *A practical guide to reciprocal teaching* (pp. 34, 39). Bothell, WA: Wright Group/McGraw-Hill; adapted by permission.

Getting Into Words: Vocabulary Instruction that Strengthens Comprehension by Shira Lubliner (with Linda Smetana)

Name: _____ Date: _____

ALL IN THE FAMILY

*Word families are groups of words that are related to the same base word. If you know the base word, it is easy to find all of the relatives. Just look inside the word! In the example below, we read the story in the box and underline the words that belong to the **send** family. We write each word in the **send** family in the circle.*

SEND

sent
sends
sending
sender

I need to <u>send</u> a birthday card to my grandma. She always <u>sends</u> me a card and a present for my birthday. Last year I <u>sent</u> the card to the wrong address. It came back to me with the label returned to <u>sender</u>. This year I'm <u>sending</u> Grandma two cards, just in case I make a mistake!

*Read the story in the box below. Underline the words that are part of the **build, work,** and **employ** word families, and write them in the family circles.*

Ever since he was a little boy, Jason was interested in his dad's work. Jason's dad owned a construction company that built houses and apartments. He employed six workers who helped him. Jason always wanted to be a builder like his dad. He begged his dad to take him to work. But his dad said that a construction site was too dangerous for small children.

When Jason turned 10, his dad finally agreed to take him to work. On the first day of winter break, Jason and his dad went to see the new apartment house the company was building. They put on hard hats to protect their heads. Dad helped Jason climb into the lift that took them to the third floor. Dad had to discuss some problems with the manager. Meanwhile, Jason watched the builders pounding nails into boards. "Can I help?" he asked eagerly.

The workers laughed. "Your dad is our employer, and he would fire us if you got hurt. Don't worry! You'll be old enough to work before long. Then you'll wish you were still a boy with nothing to do but play."

The workers were right. When Jason turned 16 he began working for his dad's company. He worked very hard and tried to be the perfect employee. Sometimes when he was very tired, Jason remembered how he used to beg his dad to take him to work when he was a little boy.

BUILD

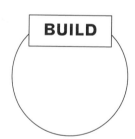

WORK

EMPLOY

Name: _____   Date: _____

PREFIX CHART

Prefixed word	Prefix	Prefix's meaning	Base word (word without prefix)	Base word's meaning	Prefixed word's meaning

WORDS WITH NEGATIVE PREFIXES

Level 4

dis-	il-, in-	mis-	un-	
disagree	illegal	misbehave	unattached	unlikely
disappear	incomplete	misfortune	unattractive	unlucky
disapprove	incorrect	misjudge	uncertain	unnecessary
discomfort	independence	misplace	unchanged	unpleasant
disconnect	insane	mistreat	unclean	unprepared
discover	invisible	misunderstand	undisturbed	unprotected
dislike			unexpected	unready
disobey			unexplored	unreasonable
displease			unfair	unsafe
			unfinished	unseen
			unfriendly	unskilled
			unhappy	untrue
			unharmed	unwanted
			unheard of	unwelcome
			unimportant	unwilling
			uninteresting	unwise
			unkind	unworthy
			unknown	unwritten

Level 6

dis-	il-, in-	mis-	un-	
discontented	inability	misfit	unable	unlike
displace	inaccurate	misinformation	unaware	unlock
dissimilar	incapable	mislead	unbearable	unorganized
	inconsiderate	mismanage	uncivilized	unsteady
	incredible	mispronounce	unconquered	unsuccessful
	incurable	mistrust	unconscious	untidy
	indescribable		uncover	unusual
	ineffective		uneasy	unwanted
	inexact		unfortunate	unwise
	inexperienced		unidentified	unworthy
	innumerable		uninjured	

Source: Dale & O'Rourke, 1981.

Getting Into Words: Vocabulary Instruction that Strengthens Comprehension
by Shira Lubliner (with Linda Smetana)

ATTITUDE ADJUSTMENT

Harry has a bad attitude. He adds a negative prefix to almost everything he says. This is Harry's letter to you.

Dear Classmate,

I dislike you because you are very unkind to me. Your unpleasant attitude makes me very unhappy.

I dislike all of the other kids in my class, too. They are unable to follow the rules in the games we play. This makes me quite displeased. Their behavior is inappropriate, and I am usually unable to enjoy being in the class.

I really dislike my teacher, Mr. Jones. He has unrealistic expectations of us, and I always misunderstand his directions. His explanations are illogical, and I am discontented in his class.

I also dislike my family, particularly my brother, Sam. His clothing is distasteful and he always behaves inappropriately. He is completely unreliable, and that makes me feel very uncomfortable. I wish he would disappear sometime soon.

I especially dislike my dog, Max. He has a very unpleasant smell and looks unappealing. Max is so unintelligent that he is incapable of doing tricks. Max is disloyal to me and disappears as soon as I come home from school each day. I really disagree that dogs are a man's best friend.

I am a very unhappy kid because I have the most disagreeable friends and the most disreputable family in the world.

Insincerely yours,

Harry

*Help give Harry an attitude adjustment! Delete the negative prefixes **un-**, **il-**, **in-**, and **dis-** from his letter. Read the letter again. Does Harry sound nicer without the negative prefixes?*

LATIN ROOT LIST

ROOT	WHAT IT MEANS	EXAMPLE
dict	to say	contradict (say something against)
equ	the same	equal (having the same value or quality)
fac/fact/fect	to do, to make	factory (a place where things are made)
form	shape	deformed (misshapen)
ject	throw	eject (to throw out)
jud/jur/jus	judge	prejudice (negative judgment about people)
loc	place	location (a place)
man	hand	manual (by hand)
mem	remember	memorize (learn something by heart)
port	to carry	transport (to carry from place to place)
prim/prin	first	primary (first or most important)
ques/quer	to ask	question (something you ask)
scrib/script	to write	manuscript (a written draft of a book)
sens/sent	to feel	sensation (a feeling)
spec/spect	to look	inspect (look at very carefully)
struct	build	structure (something that has been built)
tract	drag or pull	extract (to pull out of something)
trans	across	transfer (move something from one place to another)
val	to be strong/worth	valuable (to be worth a lot)
voc	voice, to call	advocate (to voice support; a person who does so)

Getting Into Words: Vocabulary Instruction that Strengthens Comprehension
by Shira Lubliner (with Linda Smetana)
Copyright © 2005 Paul H. Brookes Publishing Co. All rights reserved.   43

GREEK ROOT LIST

ROOT	WHAT IT MEANS	EXAMPLE
astro	star	astronomy (study of the stars)
auto	self	autograph (signature by one's self)
bio	life	biology (the study of living things)
geo	earth	geology (study of the earth)
gram/graph	write, record	autograph (a written signature)
meter/metr	measure	barometer (a measure of air pressure)
micro	small	microscope (a tool that makes things look larger)
logy	study of	cardiology (study of the heart)
phil	love	Philadelphia (nicknamed "City of Brotherly Love")
phono/phon	sound	telephone (a device that carries sound a long way)
photo/phos	light	photography (taking pictures using light)
pol/polis	city, state	political (having to do with running a city or state)
phys	nature	physical (relating to the natural world)
tech/techn	art, skill	technical (requiring special skills)
tele	far	telephone (tool that allows you to talk to someone far away

Getting Into Words: Vocabulary Instruction that Strengthens Comprehension
by Shira Lubliner (with Linda Smetana)

Root _____ Origin (Greek or Latin)_____
Meaning of root _____
Word _____   Meaning _____
Word_____   Meaning _____
Word_____   Meaning _____
Word_____   Meaning _____
Word_____   Meaning _____

Getting Into Words: Vocabulary Instruction that Strengthens Comprehension
by Shira Lubliner (with Linda Smetana)
45

Name: _____   Date: _____

WORD TREE

*This word tree has words from the Latin root **spect**, which means **look**. Can you figure out what the words mean by knowing the root? Fill in the root chart below:*

inspect

respect   inspection

SPECT

Root __spect__   Origin (Greek or Latin) __Latin__
Meaning of root __look__
Word _____   Meaning _____
Word _____   Meaning _____
Word _____   Meaning _____
Word _____   Meaning _____
Word _____   Meaning _____

Grow your own word trees using your Latin and Greek word lists. Underline the root in each word and find out what it means.

Root _____   Origin (Greek or Latin) _____
Meaning of root _____
Word _____   Meaning _____
Word _____   Meaning _____
Word _____   Meaning _____
Word _____   Meaning _____
Word _____   Meaning _____

Root _____   Origin (Greek or Latin) _____
Meaning of root _____
Word _____   Meaning _____
Word _____   Meaning _____
Word _____   Meaning _____
Word _____   Meaning _____
Word _____   Meaning _____

Name: _____ Date: _____

BE A ROOT DETECTIVE

Read the text below and underline the words with Latin and Greek roots. Give the meaning of each underlined word (use your Latin and Greek root lists if you need help). Then explain the meaning of the text in your own words.

The historian was inspecting the Native American artifacts that she had found in the cave. The first thing she did was photograph each item in its original location. Then she had to extract the items from the cave very carefully so that they wouldn't be damaged. Once the artifacts were removed from the cave, the historian needed a logical way to organize them. She carefully examined each item and used scientific techniques to decide how old it was. Every artifact was dated, except for some microscopic pieces of pottery that were too difficult to work with. Once the historian dated the artifacts, she began to put them in chronological order.

The historian took careful notes about the artifacts. She wrote a detailed description of each item in her journal and dictated additional notes into her tape recorder. She planned to return to the university and write a monograph about her discovery. She was very proud to have discovered such an incredible collection of ancient Native American artifacts.

Word _____ Origin (Greek or Latin) _____ Meaning _____

Word _____ Origin (Greek or Latin) _____ Meaning _____

Word _____ Origin (Greek or Latin) _____ Meaning _____

Word _____ Origin (Greek or Latin) _____ Meaning _____

Word _____ Origin (Greek or Latin) _____ Meaning _____

Word _____ Origin (Greek or Latin) _____ Meaning _____

Word _____ Origin (Greek or Latin) _____ Meaning _____

Word _____ Origin (Greek or Latin) _____ Meaning _____

Word _____ Origin (Greek or Latin) _____ Meaning _____

Word _____ Origin (Greek or Latin) _____ Meaning _____

Word _____ Origin (Greek or Latin) _____ Meaning _____

Word _____ Origin (Greek or Latin) _____ Meaning _____

The meaning of the paragraph in my own words: _____

_____

_____

_____

Getting Into Words: Vocabulary Instruction that Strengthens Comprehension
by Shira Lubliner (with Linda Smetana)

STUDY THE STRUCTURE CUE CARD

When you find a word you don't understand, try this strategy:

STUDY THE STRUCTURE

Try to use the word's structure (how it is made) to help you. Do you know the mystery word's root? Does it have a prefix or suffix that you know? Try to use clues in the word to figure out the meaning.

Base words

Base words are building blocks that are used to make many other words. When you find a mystery word, look for the base word and see if it helps you figure out the meaning.

Roots

Many words in English have Greek or Latin roots. The root can help you figure out the meaning of the mystery word. Check your Greek and Latin root lists to find out.

Prefixes

A prefix is a beginning part that helps give a word meaning. Does the mystery word have a prefix that you know?

Suffixes

A suffix is an ending part that helps give a word meaning. Does the mystery word have a suffix that you know?

SNAPSHOT

Pretend you have a camera, and take a picture of the word and the sentence it is in so that you will remember the word the next time you see it. Each time you see the mystery word, it will be easier to remember.

Name: _____ Date: _____

BE A CONTEXT DETECTIVE

Context clues can be anywhere! Clues can be found next door, in the neighborhood, or far away. The easiest clues to find are the ones that are closest to the mystery word. But, even when clues are hard to find, good detectives don't give up! They keep on looking until they solve the mystery! (Mystery words are underlined.)

*Here is an example of a **next-door** clue:*

> The young <u>apprentice</u> was living with the printer's family and learning how to be a printer, too.

*Notice how easy this clue is to find. It is right **next door** (in the same sentence) as the mystery word.*

Explain the meaning of the mystery word: _____

_____

*This is an example of an **in-the-neighborhood** clue:*

> The ships were loaded with <u>exports</u> from the colonies. The ships sailed across the Atlantic Ocean on a trade route between Britain and the 13 colonies. Once the ships arrived in Britain, the products from the colonies were sold for a profit.

*This clue is a little harder to find. It is **in the neighborhood,** but you have to read more than one sentence to find the meaning of the mystery word.*

Explain the meaning of the mystery word: _____

_____

*Here is an example of a **far-away** clue:*

> Plantation owners grew crops such as rice, tobacco, and <u>indigo</u>. These products were called cash crops because they brought money back to the plantation when they were sold. Large plantations were able to produce cash crops because they had so many slave workers.
>
> Indigo became an important cash crop in the 1700s. People liked colorful clothing. They were willing to spend more money for cloth that was dyed blue.

*This clue requires good detective work! The meaning of the mystery word is **far away,** in the next paragraph.*

Explain the meaning of the mystery word: _____

_____

How did you use clues to figure out each kind of mystery word? _____

_____

Name: _____   Date: _____

BE A SUPER SLEUTH
Context Detective Work for Experts

How do you figure out the meaning of a word you aren't sure about? Look for the following clues that can help.

COMMA CLUES *are the easiest to figure out. The definition of the word is right there between the commas!*

EXPLANATION CLUES *can be a little more difficult when the definition is farther from the word it defines.*

FEELING CLUES *are challenging. You have to figure out the meaning of the word from all of the other information in the text.*

Look at each underlined word. Use context clues to figure out what the word means and then explain how you figured it out.

1. The Native American tribe settled on a <u>mesa</u>, a steep, flat-topped hill, hundreds of years ago. This location made the village difficult for enemies to attack.

    What does the word mean? _____

    Type of clue _____

2. The colonists were forced to pay taxes they felt were unfair. The British government did not listen to their complaints. Some colonists were so angry they didn't want to be British citizens any more. They began to think of <u>rebelling</u> against Britain.

    What does the word mean? _____

    Type of clue _____

3. Soon after the Revolutionary War Americans began to feel a sense of <u>nationalism</u>. They felt a sense of belonging to the new nation.

    What does the word mean? _____

    Type of clue _____

4. The Northwest <u>Ordinance</u> was passed in 1787. It was supposed to protect the rights of Native American tribes; however, this law did not work and the Native Americans continued to be pushed off of their land.

    What does the word mean? _____

    Type of clue _____

5. The explorers often traveled on the Ohio River or one of its <u>tributaries</u>. It was much easier to travel on the many small rivers flowing from the Ohio than it was to travel through the wilderness in the new territory.

    What does the word mean? _____

    Type of clue _____

6. There were many American settlers in Texas that wanted to be part of the United States. They wanted the government to <u>annex</u> Texas. Finally the government agreed, and Texas became a new state.

    What does the word mean? _____

    Type of clue _____

7. The new government helped people feel part of their country by choosing national <u>symbols</u> such as the American flag and the Great Seal of the United States.

    What does the word mean? _____

    Type of clue _____

8. <u>Textiles</u>, cloth goods made from cotton or wool, were produced in large factories.

    What does the word mean? _____

    Type of clue _____

Think about it!

Which sentences contain comma clues? _____

Which sentences contain explanation clues? _____

Which sentences contain feeling clues? _____

Name: _____   Date: _____

SEQUENCE SIGNAL WORDS

A **sequence chart** shows the most important things that happen in a story in the correct order. Fill in the sequence chart below with the most important things that happened in *Tale of a Tadpole*.

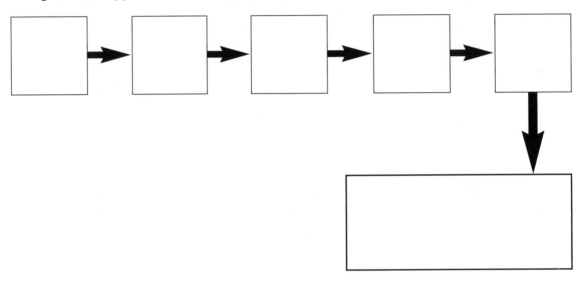

A **cloze** is a story that is missing important words. This cloze is missing sequence words that help show the order of the events in the story. Read each sentence. Pick the correct sequence word or phrase from the box below, and write in on the line so that the story makes sense. (Each word/phrase is used only once.)

Now	**Finally**	**Not long after that**	**Next**	**Then**	**First**

This is how a tadpole becomes a frog.

_____ there is a little egg in the pond.

_____ the little tadpole comes out of the egg.

_____ the tadpole grows legs and arms.

_____ , the tadpole's tail begins to shrink.

_____ the tadpole becomes a little spotted frog.

_____ the frog can breathe air like we do.

Source: Wallace, 1998.

Getting Into Words: Vocabulary Instruction that Strengthens Comprehension
by Shira Lubliner (with Linda Smetana)

Name: _____ Date: _____

COMPARE AND CONTRAST SIGNAL WORDS
Explorers and Settlers

*A **Venn diagram** shows how two things are similar and different. Begin by filling in the middle section of the Venn diagram, showing how explorers and settlers were similar. Then fill in the outside circles, showing how explorers and settlers were different.*

Explorers   **Both**   **Settlers**

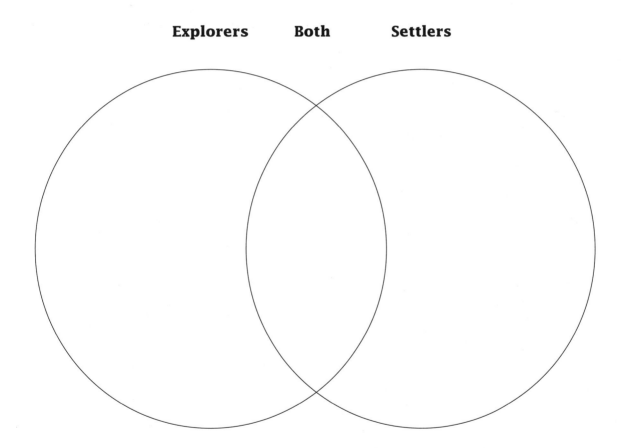

Getting Into Words: Vocabulary Instruction that Strengthens Comprehension
by Shira Lubliner (with Linda Smetana)
53

Name: _____   Date: _____

SIGNAL-WORDS CLOZE
Explorers and Settlers

A **cloze** is a text that is missing key words. Read each sentence in the cloze passage below. Find the missing word or phrase in the box (each word/phrase is used only once). Write the word/phrase on the correct line so that the story makes sense.

just like	but	alike	however	similar	different	yet

Explorers and settlers were _____ because both groups came from Europe. Explorers were _____ settlers because they did harmful things to the native people. _____, explorers were _____ from settlers because they returned to Europe.

Explorers wanted to find riches and land for the king, _____ settlers wanted to find new homes. Explorers and settlers were _____ in many ways, _____ they had very different goals.

Now, write your own **cloze,** *using compare-and-contrast signal words. See if a friend can figure out the missing words.*

_____

_____

_____

_____

_____

_____

_____

Name: _____ Date: _____

CAUSE-AND-EFFECT SIGNAL WORDS
The Little Red Hen

A **cause-and-effect** diagram shows the relationship between things that happen in a story or historical event. Let's look at the story "The Little Red Hen," for example. Write the causes (what the animals did to make the hen angry) in the first row of boxes. Then write the effect (what happened as a result) in the box on the right.

Cause-and-effect cloze: In the passage below, fill in the missing cause-and-effect signal words using words found in the box. (Each word/phrase is used only once.)

because	therefore	as a result	consequently	so that

The hen asked the animals to help her plant the wheat _____ they could have bread. She asked them to help her harvest the wheat. They refused to help. _____, the hen did it herself. She asked the animals to help her bake the bread. They would not help her. _____, the hen baked it herself. _____ she needed help and the animals would not help her, the hen got angry. _____, she ate the bread all by herself.

Think about the cause-and-effect signal words you used. Could you switch the signal words from one sentence to another? Why or why not?

_____

_____

_____

Getting Into Words: Vocabulary Instruction that Strengthens Comprehension
by Shira Lubliner (with Linda Smetana)

STOP FOR SIGNAL WORDS

 *Signal words are important clues. Stopping and thinking about signal words will help you figure out the meaning of the text.*

DEFINITION CLUES: *These signal words define something.*

refers to

means

consists of

> An American *refers* to someone who is a citizen of the United States of America.

EXAMPLE CLUES: *These signal words provide an example.*

for example

for instance

such as

including

> Many immigrants came to America to find jobs. *For instance*, they hoped to find work in American factories.

ADDITION CLUES: *These signal words show addition.*

also

another

in addition

furthermore

moreover

> Native American tribes were pushed off of their own land and forced to sign unfair treaties. *Furthermore*, they were given the worst land for reservations.

SEQUENCE CLUES: *These signal words explain the order of events.*

first

last

following

then

later

next

at that time

> *Following* the end of the Civil War, the South had to change its way of life. Plantations had to be run without slaves to do the work.

Getting Into Words: Vocabulary Instruction that Strengthens Comprehension
by Shira Lubliner (with Linda Smetana)
Copyright © 2005 Paul H. Brookes Publishing Co. All rights reserved.

COMPARISON CLUES: *These signal words compare things that are similar.*

similar

in the same way

just like

likewise

in comparison

> Explorers set out to find riches in new lands. *Likewise*, European kings hoped to gain land and treasure by supporting explorers.

OPPOSITION CLUES: *These signal words contrast things that are different.*

in contrast

on the other hand

however

whereas

but

yet

> Explorers hoped to find riches to take back to Europe. *However*, settlers were different. They hoped to build homes and stay in the new land.

CAUSE-AND-EFFECT CLUES: *These signal words show that one thing causes another.*

because

for

therefore

so

as a result

consequently

due to

thus

this led to

> The white settlers brought diseases that were deadly to the native people. *Consequently*, huge numbers of Native Americans died.

Getting Into Words: Vocabulary Instruction that Strengthens Comprehension
by Shira Lubliner (with Linda Smetana)
Copyright © 2005 Paul H. Brookes Publishing Co. All rights reserved.

CONSIDER THE CONTEXT CUE CARD

When you find a word you don't understand, try this strategy:

CONSIDER THE CONTEXT

Read the sentence. Does it give you a clue about the word's meaning? Read the whole paragraph. Now can you tell what the word means? Don't give up! You may need to read further to find information about the word. Use the following context clues to help you.

Look for comma clues.

Context clues sometimes hide inside double commas. Here's an example: *The <u>alien</u>, a creature from another planet, jumped out of the spaceship.* Notice that the definition of the word <u>alien</u> is inside the commas.

Look for explanation clues.

Here's an example: *The <u>shaman</u> was worried. The people of the tribe trusted him to take care of their health. But many people were sick and his medicine wasn't working.* Notice that the word <u>shaman</u> is explained by the sentences that follow.

Look for feeling clues.

Here's an example: *Last night I was <u>terrified</u>. I was home alone when the storm began. The lights went out. Lightning crashed and thunder shook the house.* Notice that word <u>terrified</u> is explained by the scary things happening in the next several sentences.

Look for opposition clues such as *but, even though, however,* and *although.*

Context clues sometimes hide. Here's an example: *I was exhausted, <u>but</u> I couldn't get any rest because of the baby's crying.* Notice that the opposition word <u>but</u> signals that a clue is hidden in the phrase following the opposition word.

Name: _____   Date: _____

FIVE STEPS
Substitute a Synonym

Substitute a Synonym *is a strategy that will help you figure out words you don't know. Look at this sentence:*

A snowy owl named Hedwig delivers Harry Potter's mail.

Let's say you don't know the word **delivers.** *Here are five steps that will help you make sense of the word.*

FIVE STEPS

1. *Mine Your Memory and try to think of the word.*
   Have you seen it in a book or heard the word before?

2. *Try to picture the word in the sentence.*
   Imagine Hedwig flying into the room and dropping an envelope in Harry's hands.

3. *Think of other words that mean the same thing.*
   (**delivers**—gives, brings)

4. *Substitute a Synonym in the sentence.*
   A snowy owl named Hedwig *brings* Harry Potter's mail.

5. *Check! Does the synonym make sense in the sentence? If it makes sense, you can continue reading. If not, try again!*
   (Yes, the synonym makes sense.)

FIVE STEPS IN ACTION

Let's try it! We'll follow the five steps to make sense of the word **habitat** *in the following sentence:*

> Hedwig lives with Harry Potter at Hogwarts,
> but snowy owls' normal habitat is in the Arctic region.

1. I think I remember reading about endangered animals' habitat—it's where they live.

2. I can picture the habitat: a cold, snowy place where snowy owls live.

3. *Habitat* means *a place where an animal lives, its home.*

4. Hedwig lives with Harry Potter at Hogwarts, but snowy owls' normal home is in the Arctic region.

5. Yes, it makes sense!

*Now you try it! Follow the five steps to figure out the meaning of the under-
lined words.*

Hedwig looks small in her cage, but snowy owls have a 5-foot <u>wingspan</u>.

1.

2.

3.

4.

5.

When enemies <u>threaten</u> Hedwig, she knows how to defend herself.

1.

2.

3.

4.

5.

Hedwig leaves her cage each night to hunt for <u>prey</u>.

1.

2.

3.

4.

5.

*Write four sentences of your own. Include a hard word in each sentence and
underline it. Switch papers with a partner. Follow the five steps to figure out
the meaning of the words in your partner's sentences.*

1.

2.

3.

4.

Chapter 3

Clarifying Strategies in Action

Teaching children to implement clarifying strategies spontaneously and flexibly during reading takes a great deal of carefully designed instruction. The following instructional framework can be used to organize clarifying strategy instruction (Gambrell et al., 1999; Lubliner, 2001; Palincsar, 1983, 1985; Pearson & Dole, 1987; Pressley et al., 1995):

- *Access prior knowledge:* Discuss the content of the text before reading, using pictures and examples if important concepts are unfamiliar.

- *Provide a rationale for instruction:* Explain to children that learning this particular strategy will help them understand what they read and perform better in school.

- *Use explicit instruction, including modeling and thinking aloud:* Provide careful instruction, teaching children exactly how to select and implement the clarifying strategy. Model the process using examples with a range of texts. Demonstrate how to think aloud so that children can view the internal process of proficient strategy implementation.

- *Scaffold instruction:* Use the Tools of Success, such as cue cards (see pp. 38, 48, and 58), and concrete symbols to help children understand abstract ideas. Gradually withdraw scaffolds as students gain understanding and internalize new strategic skills.

- *Guide practice:* Ask students to try the new strategy with your help. Encourage them to work with partners and to support one another as they practice the strategy. Provide coaching and encouragement to the children as they work.

- *Release responsibility:* Encourage children to implement the strategy during independent reading and acknowledge their efforts and success.

Following is a snapshot of a clarifying strategy lesson based on the instructional framework. The lesson was designed to help children select and implement appropriate clarifying strategies with unfamiliar words encountered in a text.

Model Lesson: Mrs. Green's Class

"Hi, Dr. Lubliner!" The third graders greeted me enthusiastically. I was a regular visitor at Blackwood Elementary School, working with teachers to strengthen their literacy instruction. I had modeled several strategy lessons in Mrs. Green's class over the past few months, so the children and I knew each other well. Mrs. Green assured me that she had worked hard on the clarifying strategies (see Chapter 2) and that the children were ready for action. I passed out copies of the book *Monsters of the Deep* (Blake, 1996) and asked the children to take out their Clarifying Cue Card (see p. 38). I pointed to the enlarged version of this cue card posted on the classroom wall and reviewed the strategies: Mine Your Memory, Study the Structure, Consider the Context, and Substitute a Synonym. I was pleased that the children seemed to be quite familiar with these strategies.

Dr. Lubliner: Now that you all remember the clarifying strategies we learned last time, I have a question for you: Why do we need these strategies?

Tara: To help us read better?

Dr. Lubliner: Right! Strategies help people learn words, which makes it easier to understand books. These are the same strategies that grown-ups use when they have to read hard books and articles.

Ben: My dad always tells me to look it up when I find a word I don't know.

Dr. Lubliner: I can't believe it! That's exactly what my dad used to tell me too! (Children laugh.) Dictionaries are fine, but when you're reading and you don't want to spend a lot of time looking up a word, clarifying strategies work a lot better. So, if you learn to use clarifying strategies, you'll only need to use the dictionary for the really hard words.

Okay, let's get started! Today we'll be working with one of my favorite books (holds up *Monsters of the Deep*). We're going to use the book to practice the clarifying strategies. I'm going to start by reading the first paragraph on page 2. I'll try to find the hard words, and then I'll use the clarifying strategies on the Clarifying Cue Card to help me figure out what the words mean. I want you to follow along in your books and listen very carefully. (Reads)

Much of the world under the water is alien to us. Large areas of the world's oceans and seas remain unexplored—deep, dark, and mysterious. (Blake, 1996, p. 2)

(Thinks aloud) Hmm... I need to pick out the hard words and clarify them. I think that *alien* is a hard word. Now, which strategy can I use to clarify the word? I know! (Points to the first strategy on the chart) I can mine my memory to see if I've ever seen or heard the word before. *Alien....* Let's see.... I think I remember seeing *aliens* from outer space on TV. They're strange little space men. So, I think alien must be something strange. Now, I'll substitute the synonym *strange* to make sure I understand the word (substitutes the word and reads the sentence): Much of the world under the water is *strange* to us. Yes, I think that makes sense.

Now, who can explain what I just did?

Joon-Rae: You figured out the word.

Dr. Lubliner: How did I do it?

Joon-Rae: You mined your memory. You remembered what you knew about aliens from outer space.

Dr. Lubliner: That's right! What else did I do?

Alison: You used another word to check and it worked!

Dr. Lubliner: Great! Now, this time I'm going find a hard word and we'll practice clarifying it step by step. Let's see...I think *unexplored* is a hard word. I'll look at the Clarifying Cue Card (points to the chart) and find the best strategy to help me figure it out. I always try Mine Your Memory first to see if I know the word. But this time it doesn't work because I can't remember anything about the word *unexplored*. So, I'll try the next strategy, Study the Structure. That means I need to look at the word parts to try to make sense of the word. I think it works! I know that *explore* means to investigate or look around and *un-* means *not*. So unexplored means that no one has looked around. Now that I have an idea of what the word means, I need to use Substitute a Synonym just to be sure. So, I'll put in the synonym *uninvestigated* and read the sentence again: Large areas of the world's oceans remain uninvestigated. Does that make sense? (Children nod.) Yes, it does!

Dr. Lubliner:	Now, I want you to help me with the next word, *mysterious*. How should we clarify this word?
Stevie:	You could use Mine Your Memory. My mom and I are reading a Harry Potter book, and a lot of things they talk about are mysterious.
Dr. Lubliner:	What do you think that means?
Stevie:	Well, Harry Potter is a wizard and lots of things that happen to him are kind of weird and scary.
Dr. Lubliner:	Good work! Stevie could mine his memory because he already knew a lot about the word *mysterious*. What would you do if you didn't already know the word?
Sarah:	You could Study the Structure, but that would only help if you knew the words inside.
Dr. Lubliner:	Which word is inside?
Sarah:	*Mystery*; I've heard it but I don't exactly know what it means.
Shobha:	I think the easiest thing is Consider the Context. You can tell that it's deep and dark, so you know it's kind of strange and scary.
Dr. Lubliner:	Great job! That's a very good way to clarify the word. Let's try Substitute a Synonym to make sure that Stevie and Shobha clarified the word correctly. Which synonym shall we use?
Kevin:	*Scary.*
Dr. Lubliner:	Okay, let's try it! Large areas of the world's oceans and seas remain unexplored—deep, dark, and scary. Do you think that works? (Children nod.) *Strange* would also work, wouldn't it? Both synonyms help us figure out that *mysterious* means *something we don't really understand and that we're a little afraid of.*
Dr. Lubliner:	You've done a great job helping me clarify the words. Now, do you understand how it works? Clarifying strategies are like tools in a toolbox. You pick the tool you need to figure out a tricky word.
Stevie:	What if the tools don't work?
Dr. Lubliner:	That happens sometimes. You try a strategy and it doesn't work. Then you try another one. (Points to the last two strategies on the cue card.)

If nothing works you can always ask a neighbor or put a Post-It in the book and look it up in the dictionary after you finish reading.

Now, it's your turn to try the clarifying strategies. I want you to read the next paragraph with your partner. Then decide which words are hard, and use your strategies to clarify them. Does everyone understand? Good! Just raise your hand if you get stuck, and Mrs. Green or I will come and help you. (Children begin working.)

Ben: (Raises his hand to ask for help) I forget what to do, and Joon-Rae doesn't know either.

Mrs. Green: How could you find out? Is there something in the room or on your desk to remind you?

Ben: Oh yeah, the cue card!

Mrs. Green: Here it is! Now let's use the Clarifying Cue Card to figure out the first word. I'll help with this one, and then you can clarify the rest of the words yourselves.

The children worked independently with partners, clarifying the challenging words in the next two paragraphs of the book. Mrs. Green and I walked around the class-

room, coaching and encouraging them as they worked. Most of the pairs were making good progress implementing the clarifying strategies, though they still needed more practice to become proficient, independent word learners. I wrapped up the lesson with a brief discussion, allowing the children to share comments about the experience. Most of the children reported that clarifying was fun and expressed confidence that they "did it right." I concluded by reminding them to use the clarifying strategies every time they read.

The model lesson in Mrs. Green's class illustrates a number of points about clarifying strategy instruction. Children need explicit instruction with a great deal of modeling in order to learn how strategies work. The teacher guides the children through their initial attempts at implementing clarifying strategies and provides a cue card as a scaffold to support learning. Gradually, the teacher withdraws support and allows the children to assume responsibility for their own learning. Children work together on clarifying strategy activities so that they can learn from each other. The teacher reminds the children frequently to use strategies during independent reading. A variety of instructional texts are used for strategy instruction, helping children develop skills that transfer across the curriculum.

The success of clarifying strategy lessons is dependent on a range of factors, including careful teacher preparation and well-designed instructional texts. The importance of these factors were highlighted by my visit later that day to Mr. Bradshaw's class.

Model Lesson: Mr. Bradshaw's Class

Mr. Bradshaw approached me in the lunchroom and asked if I would model a clarifying strategy lesson based on his third-grade science textbook. I had not scheduled any lessons after lunch, so I agreed to visit his class. When the bell rang, I accompanied Mr. Bradshaw to his classroom. He quickly posted an enlarged version of the Clarifying Cue Card (see Figure 2.1) on the wall and introduced me to the children. I handed out copies of the cue card and demonstrated how to use each of the strategies. The children caught on quickly, and I was pleased with their response to instruction. I decided that it was time to model the strategies with the book that Mr. Bradshaw provided. I had not seen this particular book before, but I assumed that it would work well.

"You did a great job with the Clarifying Cue Card, everyone! Now let's open your science books to page 54 and see how the clarifying strategies work with words in a book."

The children opened up their books and searched for the page. "Okay, let's get started. I'll read aloud and you follow along in your books. When we come to a hard word we'll stop and use our strategies."

I began reading the first paragraph of the text and stopped at the word *evolution*. Unfortunately, the definition of *evolution* was enclosed in parentheses immediately after the word. "Can anyone tell me how we could figure out this word?" I asked.

One of the girls raised her hand, "It says what it means right here!" she said, pointing to the book.

"I know. But how could we figure it out if the definition were not there?" I asked.

The children looked puzzled. It was clearly beyond their capacity to clarify a word that was already defined. So, we continued reading the text. Nearly all of the hard words were accompanied by definitions, which made it very difficult to implement clarifying strategies. However, the textbook provided definitions only once. When the children encountered the difficult words again, there was no information in the text to support comprehension.

"Look boys and girls, here's the word *evolution* again. Can anyone mine their memory and tell me what it means?"

The children stared at me blankly. I realized that they did not remember having read the definition and had not acquired even partial word knowledge. We tried the clarifying strategy Consider the Context and were able to construct word meaning that the children were far more likely to remember.

The experience in Mr. Bradshaw's class taught me several valuable lessons. I realized that despite my status as an expert teacher, I could not simply walk into a classroom unprepared and teach clarifying strategies effectively. I decided that in the future I would not accept last-minute requests for model lessons that did not allow me the time to preview the textbooks and prepare materials. My experience underscored the fact that effective instruction requires careful preparation.

I also gave a great deal of thought to the problem I encountered with the textbook. The inclusion of definitions immediately following the difficult words was intended to support comprehension but actually seemed to inhibit the children's word-learning proficiency. The third graders were unable to use strategies in the presence of definitions, and they did not retain definitional information that supported comprehension. The clarifying method was at odds with the goals of the textbook publisher, and the textbook trumped the method!

When teachers design clarifying strategy lessons, they need to look for texts that are not *too* considerate. When definitions and pictures accompany every challenging word, the children do not have to work at word learning. Consequently, they are unable to comprehend the textbook when the words appear again without supporting information. Clarifying strategy lessons should be based on texts that include challenging words and ample opportunities for strategy use because these text characteristics are likely to support vocabulary acquisition and reading comprehension.

Part III

Developing
Metacognitive Skills

Chapter 4

Traffic Signs, Word Knowledge, and Self-Monitoring

"Mommy, why are you stopping?" my daughter once asked. We were on our way to preschool, and I had just pulled to a stop in front of a large red stop sign. Three-year-old Dania (now grown up and a teacher herself) was intrigued by the power of the stop sign to regulate my driving behavior. I explained the importance of traffic signs and signals, telling her that these devices ensure that we follow the traffic laws that keep us safe. I reminded her of the rules we had talked about: "Stop at the red light!" "Look both ways before crossing!" Traffic signs and signals were a familiar part of her world, a set of symbols she already understood at the age of 3.

In this chapter, several instructional activities based on traffic signs and signals are introduced. These devices scaffold instruction because they are concrete symbols that children understand. Children know that traffic signs and signals regulate our movement, warning us about speed limits and hazards and ordering us to stop, turn, go, and so forth. The stop sign serves a similar purpose when used to teach word comprehension skills. It provides children with a symbolic representation of the cognitive process of stopping when one does not understand a word in a text. Teachers use the symbolic activities described in this chapter to scaffold children's understanding of complex metacognitive skills. Gradually, children begin to internalize self-regulating skills and no longer need the concrete symbols used for instruction. By the time they are adults, good readers have fully internalized self-regulating behaviors that promote reading proficiency.

Imagine that you, a proficient adult reader, are reading a book and encounter the following passage:

> Mark rushed through the corridor, his thoughts consumed by the scoritome. When he reached the classroom door, he paused for a moment, caught his breath and entered the room.

Did you stop when you read the pseudoword *scoritome?* What thoughts went through your mind as you realized you did not know the word? Some people describe the experience of reading as an internal movie, with a series of pictures flashing through the mind at lighting speed. When an unknown word is encountered, the screen goes blank, signaling the need for reparative action. The blank screen that jars the mind into action provides evidence of the proficient reader's metacognitive skills.

You probably stopped when you became aware that you did not know the pseudoword *scoritome.* Now, reflect for a moment on how you solved the problem of the unknown word. Which strategies did you use? Did you quickly try memory and discover the word was not in your personal lexicon? You probably reread the passage and used context to try to figure out the meaning of the word. Good readers know what to do. They use powerful metacognitive skills to monitor comprehension and to determine when strategies are needed to restore comprehension.

METACOGNITION AND VOCABULARY

Metacognitive knowledge is defined as awareness of one's own cognitive processes, that is, thinking about thinking. It entails *self-monitoring,* the ability to monitor one's own learning, and *self-regulation,* the ability to implement strategies to achieve cognitive goals. Words are the smallest units of verbal thought, building blocks of meaning (Vygotsky, 1978). Monitoring word knowledge is an integral part of monitoring comprehension of texts. Good readers appear to use a self-monitoring device to track comprehension as they read. When they encounter an unknown word, the self-monitoring device acts as a stop sign, signaling the need to repair the problem. Children and less proficient adult readers do not appear to have functioning self-monitoring devices to track comprehension. When they come across an unknown word while reading, they keep reading, unaware that a problem exists. Often they continue to read, skipping unfamiliar words without taking reparative action. If this pattern continues, comprehension breaks down and meaning is lost.

FALLING OFF THE PAGE

Sometimes comprehension breaks down, and the reader continues to skim the surface of the text. This process of losing meaning can be called *falling off the page.* All of us experience this phenomenon from time to time, due to lack of interest, distraction, or other factors. Good readers quickly realize that they have fallen off the page and take action to restore comprehension. This metacognitive behavior, however, is not an innate skill for many readers. Explicit instruction is necessary if children are to learn to continually monitor comprehension and to take reparative action when they fall off the page.

INTENTIONAL WORD LEARNING DURING READING

Researchers agree that most vocabulary is acquired through incidental word learning, defined as acquiring vocabulary during reading without conscious effort or instruction (Baker, 1995; Fukkink & de Glopper, 1998; Nagy, 1988; Nagy & Herman, 1984). Incidental word learning, however, is a very inefficient process and results in only a 5% chance of a given word being learned in any particular encounter with a text (Nagy, 1985). The purpose of this chapter is to reduce children's reliance on incidental vocabulary acquisition by providing them with the skills to become intentional word learners. When children internalize effective clarifying strategies and use them intentionally, word learning during reading can be substantially improved.

The process of intentional word learning looks like this: A child reads a text, monitoring word comprehension. She encounters an unknown word, assesses her level of word knowledge, and determines that reparative action is necessary. She attempts to understand the unknown word, possibly trying several clarifying strategies before meaning is constructed. This intentional word learning process provides her with multiple opportunities to acquire new vocabulary.

TEACHING CHILDREN METACOGNITIVE SKILLS

Children must internalize an array of metacognitive skills if they are to become efficient word learners. The first task is to teach children that the purpose of reading is to make meaning of a text. The centrality of meaning making in the reading process seems obvious to good readers, but many children who lack reading proficiency are completely unaware of this basic concept. In fact, many children say that good reading is "saying words fast and right." They identify fluency and accuracy, rather than the extraction of meaning from a text, as the essence of good reading. The current emphasis on developing reading fluency may exacerbate this problem. Unless teachers are careful to emphasize the importance of understanding, rather than focusing narrowly on speed and accuracy, children may miss the essential nature and purpose of reading proficiency.

MONITORING WORD KNOWLEDGE

Stop Sign

Teachers begin metacognitive instruction by teaching children to think as they read and to monitor their own word comprehension. The Stop Sign activity is used as the basis of instruction. The red paper stop sign used in this activity is a visual tool, reminding children of the need to stop for unknown words. (Teachers cut stop signs out of red construction paper and mount them on Popsicle sticks.)

The following snapshot of Stop Sign takes place in a third-grade class that includes a number of struggling readers. In a prior lesson, the teacher, Ms. Ames, had introduced the text *The Great Race* (Brocker, 2000) and developed background knowledge by showing pictures of Alaskan sled dogs. She read the story and discussed it with the students. Ms. Ames is now preparing to read the story for the second time, with a focus on monitoring word knowledge. The snapshot begins as she models identifying unknown words in sentence.

Ms. Ames's Class

Ms. Ames: Boys and girls, I want you to listen carefully as I read this sentence:

John went home after school and started his homework.

What were you thinking when I read the sentence?

Tenisha: About a boy doing his homework.

Ms. Ames: Right! Did anyone have a picture of John in his or her mind?

Drew: Yeah! I pictured him sitting at a table like the one where I do my home-work.

Mara: I pictured him walking home and sitting on his bed doing homework like I do.

Ms. Ames: Good! We all use our own experiences when we read. We make mean-ing out of the story that way. Now listen to this sentence:

                John went home after school and started his opus.

                What happened when I read the word *opus*?

Tenisha: I didn't know it.

Ms. Ames: What thoughts went through your head?

Tenisha: Nothing.... I didn't have any thoughts because I don't know what *opus* is.

Ms. Ames: That's exactly right! When you don't know a word, your mind goes blank. When that happens you need to stop reading and do something to fig-ure out the word. So, tell me to stop reading like this! (She models lifting the stop sign.) If you do this every time you don't understand a word, it will help you a lot. You'll start to pay attention to words you don't know, and then you'll learn them.

                Now, I'm going to read *The Great Race* (Brocker, 2000). We read the story yesterday and looked at pictures of sled dogs. Remember? (Stu-dents nod.) Today we're going to read it again and just focus on the hard words in the story. Watch what I do! I'm going to pretend that I'm one of you. I'll start reading on page 18, and when I come to a word that I don't understand I'll use my stop sign like this (lifts stop sign). (Begins reading)

Balto, the sled dog, plunged through the roaring blizzard...

(Stops reading, lifts the stop sign, and begins to think aloud) *Plunged* ...hmm...I could see the sled dog in my mind as I was reading. I came to the word *plunged*, and my mind went blank. So I raised my stop sign and tried to figure out the word *plunged*... Oh, I think I remember that word. I read in our science book that the sea lions plunged into the water when they were afraid. So, I think *plunged* means *jumped in*, or something like that. Let's check. *Balto, the sled dog jumped into the roaring blizzard....* Yes, it makes sense....

Does everyone understand what I just did? (Students nod.) First I lifted the stop sign to show that the word *plunged* was unfamiliar. I mined my memory and figured out what the word meant. Then I substituted a synonym to make sure that the meaning made sense.

Now I want you to follow along in your books and try to picture the words in your head as I read. When I read a word you don't know, lift up your stop sign. I'll stop reading and we'll figure out what the word means. (Reads slowly from the text)

On January 20, 1925, a radio signal went out across the frozen land of Alaska. It was an urgent...

Josh: Stop! (Raises his stop sign) I don't get that word you read.

Ms. Ames: *Urgent?* (Josh nods.) Does anyone know what the word means?

Tenisha: It means *very important*, doesn't it?

Ms. Ames: Yes, you're right, Tenisha. And great job, Josh! That's exactly what I want you to do. Each time you hear a word you don't know lift up your stop sign. Now that we understand the word *urgent*, we can go on with the

story. (She continues reading. The children lift their stop signs whenever Ms. Ames reads an unknown word.)

The students in this snapshot were struggling readers who had not learned to monitor word knowledge or reading comprehension in the early grades. Ms. Ames was determined to teach them essential metacognitive skills this year. She carefully prepared for the first lesson, developing background knowledge with pictures, reading and discussing the content of the story. This ensured that the students could focus all of their cognitive resources on the metacognitive skill that she was teaching. She started her instruction with a very simple example, using a single sentence to help the children identify an unknown word. She modeled the process of signaling a loss of comprehension with the stop sign and then demonstrated the same process with a word from the text. She modeled thinking aloud to demonstrate her metacognitive processes as she dealt with an unknown word. Then she guided the students as they used the Stop Sign strategy, helping them to identify and make meaning of unknown words in the story.

In subsequent lessons, Ms. Ames encouraged the children to take more responsibility for word monitoring, assigning them to read and implement the Stop Sign strategy while reading with a partner. The students used the red paper stop signs for several weeks, gradually internalizing the metacognitive skills that would allow them to monitor word knowledge independently while reading.

Chapter 5

Word Learning and Self-Regulation

I once conducted a vocabulary development workshop with a group of elementary school teachers. We were discussing methods of building word knowledge when a fourth-grade teacher stopped me with a question: "What does it mean to know a word?" she asked. I realized that this was a very important point that teachers need to consider carefully. I explained that knowing a word might imply word recognition, receptive understanding, or expressive competence. It depends on the reader's purpose. If the reader's goal is to monitor comprehension of a text, partial word knowledge is probably sufficient. If the reader needs to understand the word and use it expressively, then full concept knowledge and syntactic control is required. Defining word knowledge is not a simple matter. Researchers have examined children's word knowledge and have determined that word learning proceeds in stages, beginning with words that are completely unknown, progressing to words that are partially known, to words that are known well and can be used independently (Dale, 1965; Graves, 1984).

WORD-LEARNING CONTINUUM

The word-learning process can be viewed as a continuum, composed of red, yellow, and green zones that represent the stages of vocabulary acquisition (see Figure 5.1). The word-learning continuum is used to identify levels of children's vocabulary knowledge. Words that fall in the red zone are easy to identify. Children do not recognize red-light words from prior exposure, nor are they familiar with any aspect of word meaning.

The yellow zone includes a broad range of words that children partially know. Yellow-light words usually reflect incomplete concept knowledge and limited ability to generalize understanding from one context to another. When a child is asked to define a yellow-light word, his response provides an indication of word-learning proficiency. At the early stages of yellow-light word learning, the child tends to generate categories or give examples to explain word meaning. For instance, he might describe a *vehicle* as *something like a car.* When asked to construct a sentence with a yellow-light word, the child may construct a syntactically correct sentence that does not reveal word meaning, such as *I have a vehicle.* Although the syntax is correct, it is impossible to determine whether the child understands the target word.

RED ZONE Red-light words	YELLOW ZONE Yellow-light words			GREEN ZONE Green-light words
I don't know the word.	I under-stand the general meaning of the word, but I can't use it.	I can give examples of the word.	I can define the word.	I know the word well and can use the word meaningfully in a sentence.
I need to stop and use clarifying strategies.	I need to slow down and check my comprehension.			I can read at the speed limit.

Figure 5.1.   The word-learning continuum.

Green-light words are characterized by full concept knowledge and expressive competence. A child who fully understands the word *vehicle,* for example, should be able to generate a sentence with clear, meaningful referents, such as the following: *My dad has a vehicle that he drives to work.* This sentence provides evidence that complete word learning has occurred.

ZONE OF UNDERSTANDING

Zone of Understanding is a self-monitoring Tool of Success based on the word-learning continuum. The teacher begins instruction by drawing a horizontal line on the board and placing a magnet next to the line. She uses colored chalk or erasable markers to underline the left part of the continuum in red, the center in yellow, and the right side in green. She carefully explains each zone and provides examples of red-light, yellow-light, and green-light words. She models the process of categorizing words and placing a magnet on the appropriate place on the continuum. The teacher first identifies a red-light word and thinks aloud as she categorizes the word as completely unknown. She indicates her lack of word knowledge by placing the magnet in the red zone. The teacher then uses clarifying strategies to construct a rough understanding of the word and then moves the magnet into the yellow zone. Finally, she demonstrates full word knowledge by using the word correctly in a sentence and moves the magnet into the green zone.

Once the teacher has modeled this process several times, she asks the children to work individually on the following task: They are asked to look at list of 10 words found in their basal reading story. They circle each word with a red, yellow,

or green crayon, colored pencil, or marker to indicate the appropriate zone of understanding. Then the teacher calls on individual children to come up to the board and move the magnet along the word-learning continuum according to their level of word knowledge. The teacher coaches the children, providing them with valuable experience in monitoring word comprehension.

READING SPEED AND WORD COMPREHENSION

Children often feel pressured to read rapidly, particularly in a group context. It is misguided to emphasize speed at the expense of comprehension. Children should not be allowed to exceed the speed limit, the pace that allows for full comprehension. When all words in a sentence are green-light words, children can read at the speed limit. When a reader encounters a yellow-light word, she needs to slow down and monitor comprehension. Often, partial word knowledge is sufficient to support comprehension and reading can proceed. When the reader comes to a red-light word, however, she needs to come to a full stop and implement clarifying strategies.

STOPLIGHT VOCABULARY

Stoplight Vocabulary is a highly effective tool that children enjoy. The teacher begins by reviewing a text that the children will be reading. She then selects challenging words and lists them next to the stoplights on the Stoplight Vocabulary Worksheet. The teacher places the Stoplight Vocabulary transparency (see p. 85) on the overhead projec-

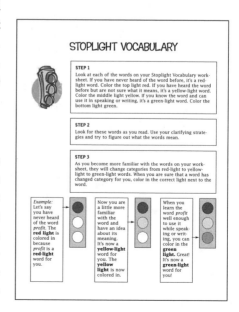

tor and explains the process. She shows the children how to color the stoplights red, yellow, or green to indicate their level of word knowledge. The teacher passes out copies of the Stoplight Vocabulary sheet (see p. 86) and explains that the words on the list are found in the text that the children will be reading. The teacher instructs the children to work independently, coloring in each stoplight to indicate their level of word knowledge. As the children complete their Stoplight Vocabulary sheets, the teacher walks around the room, noting words that the children have colored red. This provides valuable information about the students' vocabulary knowledge so that

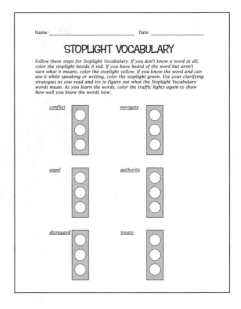

instructional time is not wasted teaching children words they already know. Children are responsible for identifying their initial word knowledge and for monitoring and changing the stoplights as word learning occurs. Page 86 shows a Stoplight Vocabulary sheet based on words found in an upper-elementary social studies textbook.

The following vignette portrays a Stoplight Vocabulary lesson based on the Stoplight Vocabulary sheet on page 86. Fifth-grade teacher Mr. Mason has selected words from a unit on explorers that he thinks will be difficult for the students. While preparing the Stoplight Vocabulary sheet for students, he made a transparency of the sheet.

Mr. Mason's Class

Mr. Mason: Okay folks, I'm going to pretend to be a student. I'm looking at a list of tough words (points to the Stoplight Vocabulary sheet, on page 86, displayed on the overhead projector) that are in this unit of the social studies book. I'm going to think aloud for you as I decide what to do about the first word on this Stoplight Vocabulary sheet.

The first word is *conflict*. Let's see…. The first thing I need to do is decide if I know this word at all. I think I've heard it before, and it has something to do with fighting. So, it definitely isn't a red-light word for me. Now the question is how well do I know this word? I can't really define it exactly and I sure can't use it in a sentence! So, I think it's a yellow-light word. (The teacher colors the stoplight next to the word *conflict* yellow.)

Now, let's look at the word *expel*. Suppose I don't know this word at all. What color do I put in the stoplight?

Kristen: Red!

Mr. Mason: Right! (Colors the stoplight next to the word *expel* red) Red is for words you don't know at all.

          Now, this next one is harder. I think I know the word *navigate* really well. How can I tell if a word should be colored green, if it's really a green-light word for me?

Brittany: You can explain about it.

Mr. Mason: That's a start. But, if you really know a word, you should be able to use it in a sentence. So, this is my sentence: *When my family takes a trip, it's my job to navigate so that we don't get lost.* Can you tell I know what the word means from this sentence? (Children nod.) Okay, so I can color the stoplight green (colors stoplight).

          Now, please look at each word on your Stoplight Vocabulary sheet and color the stoplights red, yellow, or green. I want you to think very carefully and try to be honest. This is only going to help you learn if you color in the stoplights based on what you really know. Okay? Let's get started!

As the children color in the stoplights, Mr. Mason circulates, checking on their work. He notes words that many children have colored red and thinks that these words may require explicit instruction. He monitors the children's green-light words, asking them to construct sentences to confirm word knowledge. A number of children have to go back a level to yellow when they are unable to demonstrate thorough word knowledge. Once the children have completed their Stoplight Vocabulary sheets, the teacher calls them back together. Mr. Mason's class is now ready for the next part of the lesson, which is based on the Stoplight Vocabulary sheet shown on page 86 and the Clarifying Cue Card (p. 38), which the children use to clarify red- and yellow-light words.

Mr. Mason's Class

Mr. Mason: Now I am going to show you how to clarify the words on your Stoplight Vocabulary sheets while you read the social studies textbook. Please take out your Clarifying Cue Cards and open your social studies books to page 89. I'm going to read aloud, and I'd like you to follow along. I'll stop when I come to the first stoplight word.

(He reads a paragraph of the text and stops to clarify the first stoplight word.) *When the settlers moved west and took over more Indian land, there was increasing* conflict *with the native people.*

Let's see...*conflict*....Here's a word I colored yellow on my Stoplight Vocabulary sheet. First I'll use Mine My Memory to discover what I know about the word *conflict.* I remember that I've heard that word before—it has something to do with fighting. I don't think Study the Structure will help. So, next I'll use Consider the Context. *Conflict* seems to be about problems between the settlers and the Native Americans. I'll use Substitute a Synonym just to be sure I know this word: *When the settlers moved west and took over more Indian land there was increasing* fighting *with the native people.* Yes, that makes sense!

Now, take a look at my Stoplight Vocabulary sheet on the overhead. I've worked on this word, and I think I really know it now. So, what do I need to do?

Colin: Make a sentence with the word?

Mr. Mason: Right! Let's see....Here's my sentence: *If you follow the rules, we won't have any conflict in this classroom.* (Children laugh.) Do I understand the word really well now? (Children nod.)

Okay, I'm going to color the stoplight green because I've learned this word thoroughly (colors the stoplight next to the word *conflict* green).

Mr. Mason models clarifying another word and calls on students to demonstrate clarifying additional words with his coaching. Then he asks them to complete the activity in pairs, with each partner taking turns reading the text and clarifying the stoplight words. At the end of the activity, the children return to their Stoplight Vocabulary worksheets, reevaluating their level of word knowledge for each word and coloring in the appropriate stoplights if word learning has occurred. In the next vignette, two children finish reading and work together on their Stoplight Vocabulary sheets (see p. 86).

Mr. Mason's Class

Kristen: (Finishes reading the last paragraph in the chapter) That's it! We're done!

Brittany: Not yet! We're supposed to go back and change the colors on the stop-lights now...if we learned anything about the words.

Kristen: Okay, you want to go first?

Brittany: Yeah! I'll do *conflict*. I colored it yellow.

Kristen: Can you make it green?

Brittany: Yeah, Mr. Mason showed us that one: *If you follow the rules, we won't have any* conflict *in this classroom.* See, it's green! (Colors stoplight green)

Kristen: (Laughs at Brittany's example and colors the stoplight beside *conflict* green on her own worksheet)

Brittany: Wait! You can't color it too. You have to make your own sentence.

Kristen: Well, you used the teacher's sentence.

Brittany: Yeah, but you let me go first!

Kristen: Okay, okay, here's your sentence: *I have a* conflict *with you right now.*

Brittany: (Laughs) Okay, color it green! Let's do a new one. How about *disregard?* I colored it red the first time.

Kristen: I colored it green.

Brittany: You did? Then make a sentence with it.

Kristen: I like *disregard.*

Brittany: (Argumentatively) That doesn't count. You can't tell what the word means in your sentence.

Kristen: (Raises her voice) Yes you can!

Mr. Mason: (Hears the girls arguing and comes over to help) What's the problem, girls?

Brittany: She colored *disregard* green, but her sentence doesn't count because you can't tell what the word means.

Mr. Mason: What's your sentence, Kristen?

Kristen: Uh...I guess it's not green (crosses out the green circle). I'll make it yellow.

Mr. Mason: Can you tell me something about the word *disregard,* Kristen?

Kristen: Well, in the book it made sense. It was something like not caring about the Indians.

Mr. Mason: Great! That's a perfect example of a yellow-light word. You can understand it in context, but you don't fully know the word yet. Good work, girls!

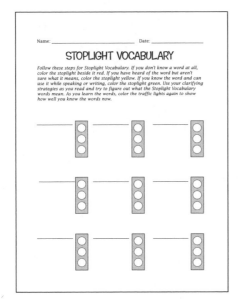

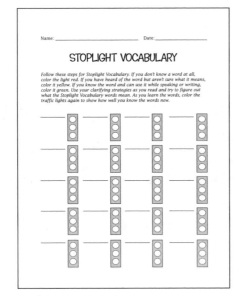

This snapshot illustrates the importance of providing opportunities for children to work together on metacognitive activities. When Mr. Mason was talking about the word *conflict*, he did almost all of the talking. The students were relatively passive recipients of his instruction. When he grouped the children into pairs and asked them to work cooperatively on the assignment, the quantity of student speech rose substantially. Although the children needed explicit instruction in this metacognitive task, they also benefited from the opportunity to discuss words with a peer and to try their emerging word-learning skills.

A set of Stoplight Vocabulary instructional materials is provided on the following pages. The teacher's transparency master (see p. 85) is used for modeling the process that has been described in this chapter. Two versions of student Stoplight Vocabulary sheets (see pp. 87–88) are instructional tools that teachers can adapt for the grade and proficiency level of the students. The version with fewer stoplights (see p. 87) is suitable for younger children and struggling readers. Older children and more proficient readers benefit from the larger number of stoplights on the advanced version shown on page 88.

STOPLIGHT VOCABULARY

STEP 1

Look at each of the words on your Stoplight Vocabulary worksheet. If you have never heard of the word before, it's a red-light word. Color the top light red. If you have heard the word before but are not sure what it means, it's a yellow-light word. Color the middle light yellow. If you know the word and can use it in speaking or writing, it's a green-light word. Color the bottom light green.

STEP 2

Look for these words as you read. Use your clarifying strategies and try to figure out what the words mean.

STEP 3

As you become more familiar with the words on your worksheet, they will change categories from red-light to yellow-light to green-light words. When you are sure that a word has changed category for you, color in the correct light next to the word.

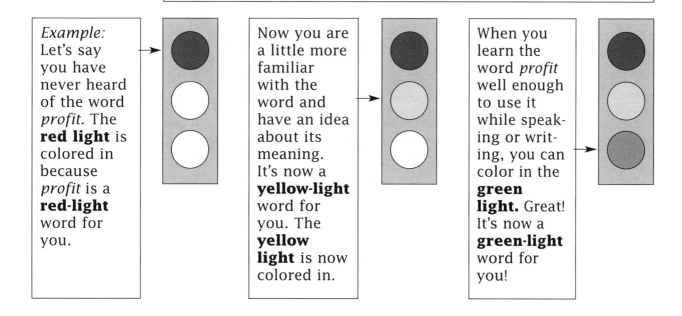

Example: Let's say you have never heard of the word *profit.* The **red light** is colored in because *profit* is a **red-light** word for you.

Now you are a little more familiar with the word and have an idea about its meaning. It's now a **yellow-light** word for you. The **yellow light** is now colored in.

When you learn the word *profit* well enough to use it while speaking or writing, you can color in the **green light.** Great! It's now a **green-light** word for you!

Getting Into Words: Vocabulary Instruction that Strengthens Comprehension by Shira Lubliner (with Linda Smetana)

Name: _____   Date: _____

STOPLIGHT VOCABULARY

Follow these steps for Stoplight Vocabulary. If you don't know a word at all, color the stoplight beside it red. If you have heard of the word but aren't sure what it means, color the stoplight yellow. If you know the word and can use it while speaking or writing, color the stoplight green. Use your clarifying strategies as you read and try to figure out what the Stoplight Vocabulary words mean. As you learn the words, color the traffic lights again to show how well you know the words now.

conflict   navigate

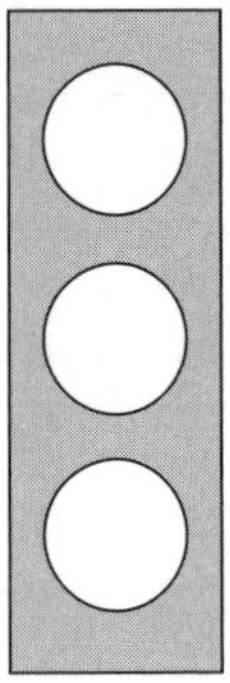

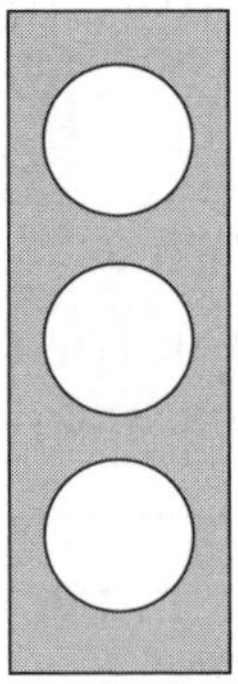

expel 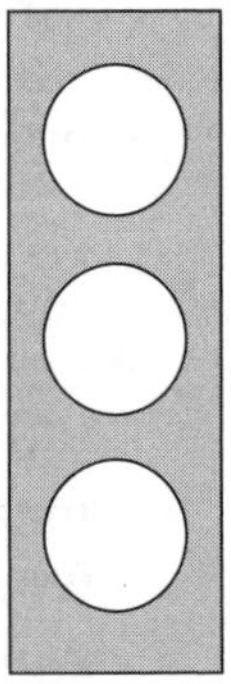   authority

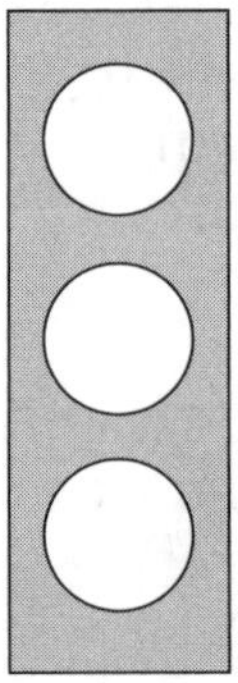

disregard 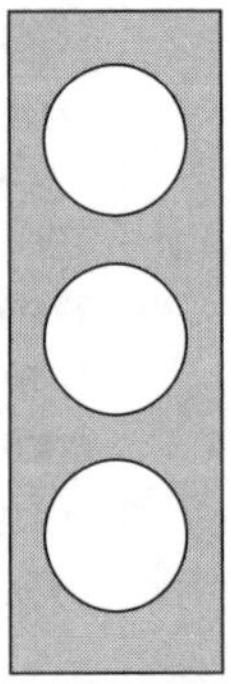   treaty

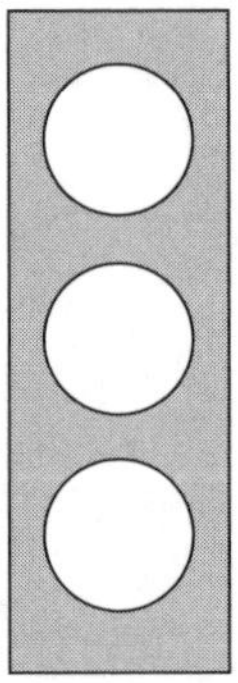

Getting Into Words: Vocabulary Instruction that Strengthens Comprehension
by Shira Lubliner (with Linda Smetana)

86

Name: _____ Date: _____

STOPLIGHT VOCABULARY

Follow these steps for Stoplight Vocabulary. If you don't know a word at all, color the stoplight beside it red. If you have heard of the word but aren't sure what it means, color the stoplight yellow. If you know the word and can use it while speaking or writing, color the stoplight green. Use your clarifying strategies as you read and try to figure out what the Stoplight Vocabulary words mean. As you learn the words, color the traffic lights again to show how well you know the words now.

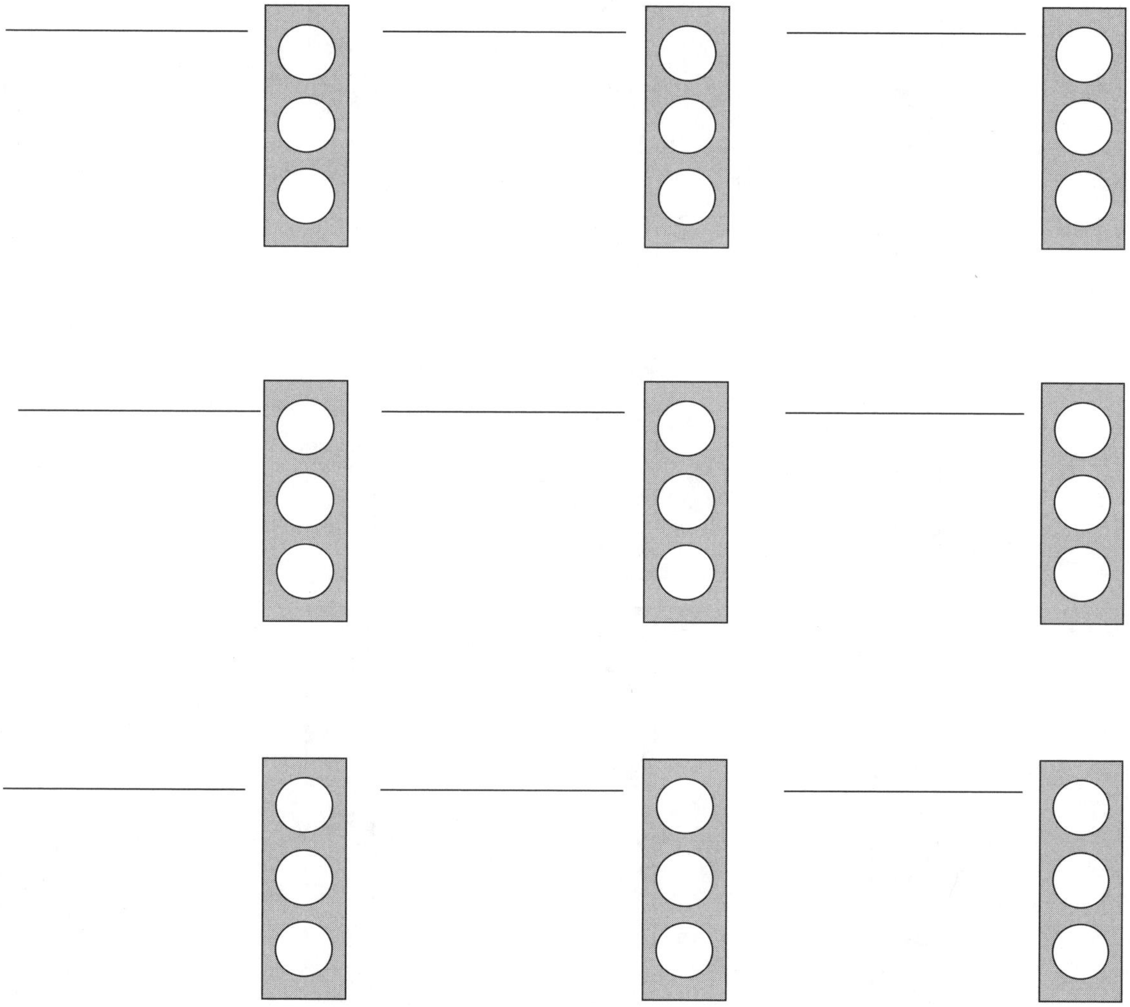

Name: _____   Date: _____

STOPLIGHT VOCABULARY

Follow these steps for Stoplight Vocabulary. If you don't know a word at all, color the light red. If you have heard of the word but aren't sure what it means, color it yellow. If you know the word and can use it while speaking or writing, color it green. Use your clarifying strategies as you read and try to figure out what the Stoplight Vocabulary words mean. As you learn the words, color the traffic lights again to show how well you know the words now.

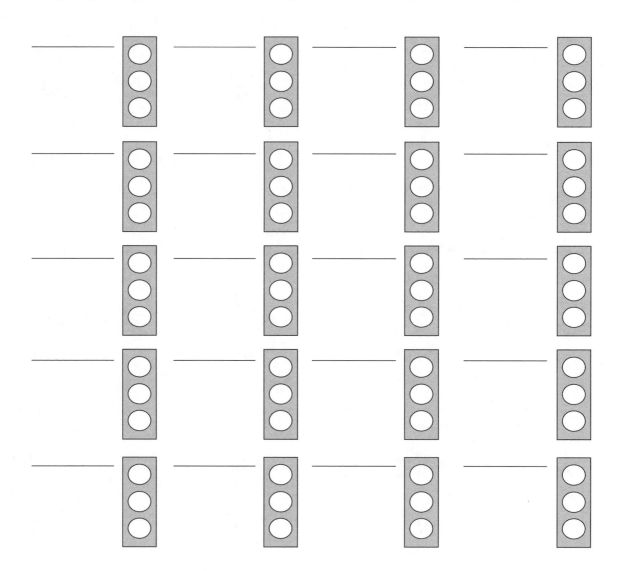

Chapter 6

Controlling Word-Learning Strategies

Now that children know the clarifying strategies and can accurately identify their levels of word learning, they are ready for another level of skill in the conditional dimension: self-regulation of strategic knowledge. Self-regulation entails selecting the most appropriate strategy or strategies to clarify unknown words, checking to make sure the constructed meaning makes sense, and responding flexibly when a strategy does not work.

Teaching children to regulate the use of clarifying strategies is a complex undertaking. Children often expect to be given rules such as math formulas and expect the rules to work consistently in producing the desired outcome. Clarifying involves a different set of expectations. A clarifying strategy must be understood as a heuristic, an approach to problem solving that may or may not work, rather than as an algorithm that is guaranteed to produce a solution. Children must develop persistence in applying strategies and a tolerance for frustration when strategies are not effective. Explicit instruction helps children develop the metacognitive skills necessary to manage strategies effectively. The following dialogue takes place in a sixth-grade classroom as the teacher, Mrs. Miller, guides the students in acquiring conditional strategic skills.

Mrs. Miller's Class

Mrs. Miller: (Points to the Clarifying Cue Card [see p. 38] chart on the wall) We've been working on the clarifying strategies for quite a while, and you know them pretty well. Today we're going to look at the strategies more closely and decide how they should be used. Take a look at this sentence on the overhead projector:

Although they had worked well together up to this point, the boys had a disagreement over the way the final part of the project should be done.

If you weren't sure about the word *disagreement*, what is the first clarifying strategy you would try?

Justin: I'd mine my memory. I know what a disagreement is.

Mrs. Miller: Yes, most people try Mine Your Memory first. If Mine Your Memory works, then they can check themselves with Substitute a Synonym and get back to the text. Justin, which synonym would you substitute to check your understanding of this word?

Justin: Umm...argue...I think they were arguing, so I'd use the word *argument* instead of *disagreement*.

Mrs. Miller: Try it!

Justin: *Although they had worked well together up to this point, the boys had an argument over the way the final part of the project should be done.*

Mrs. Miller: Does that make sense?

Students: Yeah!

Mrs. Miller: Good! Now, let's say that you did not already know the word *disagreement*. Mine Your Memory did not work. Should you just give up and use Place a Post-It?

Erin: I think you could use Study the Structure for the word.

Mrs. Miller: Tell us how that would work!

Erin: You can see the word *agree* inside the word. If you know that *agree* is to think the same thing as someone, then you could figure out that *disagree* is to *not* think the same thing.

Mrs. Miller: That's great, Erin! Now check your understanding with Substitute a Synonym.

Erin: Okay.... *Although they had worked well together up to this point, the boys* did not think the same thing *over the way the final part of the project should be done.*

Mrs. Miller: What do you call it when people have different ideas about something? (No response) You could say that the boys had a *difference of opinion.* What about Consider the Context? Does context help clarify the word?

Justin: Not for me.

Mike: Yeah, it does. Look! (Points to the word *although* on the transparency) If you know that *although* means something different is going on, you know that at first they worked well together, but then they did not work well together anymore on the final part of the project.

Mrs. Miller: Good work, Mike! Now, I want you to think about this for a minute. Did each person clarify the word *disagreement* the same way?

Students: No!

Mrs. Miller: Right! Clarifying is different for each person because it depends on your individual word knowledge. The key point is to use the clarifying strategies flexibly so that they work for you.

Now, take a look at this sentence on the overhead:

The teacher frowned at the students as she passed back the papers, for she was very disappointed in the students' test scores.

Let's assume for a moment that you don't know the word *disappointed*. You've tried Mine Your Memory and it didn't work. Does the next strategy, Study the Structure, help?

Tania: Yeah. You can look at the prefix *dis-* and know that it means *not*.

Mrs. Miller: Not what? How does that help?

Tania: Umm...Not appointed...no, it doesn't make sense.

Erin: Study the Structure doesn't work, so you have to use Consider the Context. If you look at the word *frowned*, you know the teacher isn't happy about the tests.

Mrs. Miller: Exactly! That's what I mean by flexible. You can think of strategies as tools in your toolbox. If one doesn't do the job, you try another.

Mrs. Miller then guides the students through a number of examples, helping them to identify clarifying strategies that do and do not work with various texts. She begins with simple words so that the children's initial attempts at self-regulation will be successful. As the children gain confidence in their ability to use clarifying strategies effectively, Mrs. Miller increases the difficulty level of the vocabulary. Then she asks the students to work in pairs, clarifying a series of challenging words from their social studies textbook. As the students work, Mrs. Miller circulates, checking for understanding and coaching as needed. She is pleased to see that the students' use of the clarifying strategies is becoming more flexible.

CLARIFYING STRATEGY DECISION TREE

The most important task that the students must accomplish now is to internalize the flexible strategic skills that they have learned and apply them to independent reading. The Clarifying Strategy Decision Tree (see p. 94) provides a road map for clarifying strategy use. Each step in the process is outlined in graphic form to help children internalize the process. The purpose of this activity is to teach children to use clarifying strategies flexibly and effectively during independent reading. Since Ask an Expert is only effective when children are working in group or during full class instruction, it has not been included in the Clarifying Strategy Decision Tree.

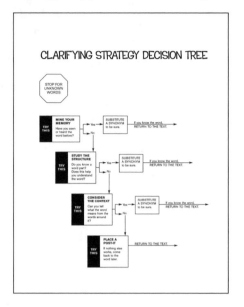

Now that Mrs. Miller has taught her students to select and implement appropriate clarifying strategies, she is ready to move to the next level of complexity. In the following snapshot, she helps her students learn to use the Clarifying Strategy Decision Tree.

Mrs. Miller's Class

Mrs. Miller: Okay, please put your books down! I'd like to talk for a minute about the clarifying strategies. How did the Clarifying Strategy Decision Tree work? Does anyone have a comment?

Rachel: I tried it. I came to this word I never saw before. I couldn't remember what to do, so I looked at the Clarifying Strategy Decision Tree.

Mrs. Miller: Did it help you?

Rachel: Yeah, sort of. I skipped Mine Your Memory because I knew I didn't know the word. The Clarifying Strategy Decision Tree said to try Study the Structure next. There weren't any word parts, so that didn't help. Then it said to try Consider the Context, and that worked.

Mrs. Miller: Good work, Rachel. Clarifying can be frustrating. You stuck with it, and your persistence paid off. You figured out the meaning of the word. Anyone else?

Juan: I got into the book and forgot to use the Clarifying Strategy Decision Tree.

Mrs. Miller: Were there any words you did not know in the chapter?

Juan: Yeah, but I could figure them out right away.

Mrs. Miller: So, you have learned the clarifying strategies so well that you use them automatically. That's great! Please put the Clarifying Strategy Decision Tree into your binders and remember to use it when you read independently. Doing this will really help you learn more words and become a better reader.

Proficient readers such as Juan quickly discard the Clarifying Strategy Decision Tree because they know what to do when they encounter an unfamiliar word during reading. Juan has already internalized effective clarifying strategies that he applies efficiently as he reads. Other children need explicit instruction and supportive tools such as the Clarifying Strategy Decision Tree to help them develop these essential metacognitive skills.

The methods included in this chapter should be incorporated into a wide range of reading activities over an extended period of time. Teaching children to monitor comprehension, learn words intentionally while reading, and apply clarifying strategies effectively will help the children become proficient independent readers.

CLARIFYING STRATEGY DECISION TREE

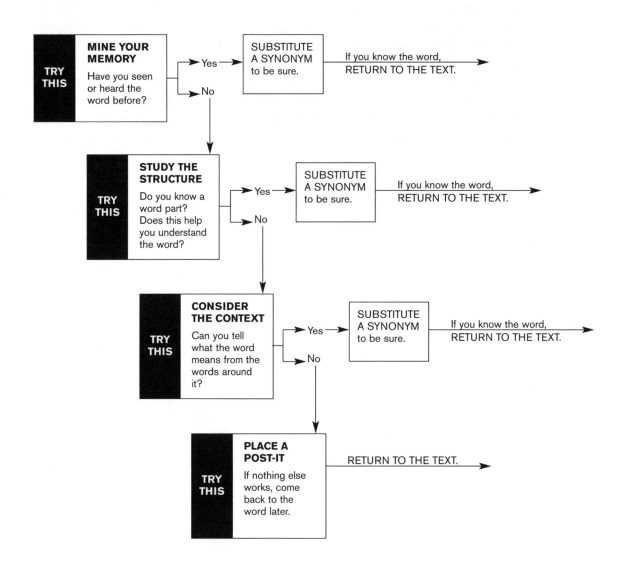

Getting Into Words: Vocabulary Instruction that Strengthens Comprehension
by Shira Lubliner (with Linda Smetana)
Copyright © 2005 Paul H. Brookes Publishing Co. All rights reserved.

94

Part IV

Building
Word Knowledge

Chapter 7

Choosing Words to Teach and Learn

One Monday morning, I was seated in a second-grade classroom in a high-achieving school. I had come to observe Jennie, who was beginning the take-over phase of her final student teaching placement. On the day of my visit, she was teaching a reading lesson based on the guidelines in the basal teacher's guide. Jennie began by preteaching the list of vocabulary words taken from the story. It was immediately apparent that Jennie's students already knew the words that she was attempting to teach them. They shouted out answers to her questions and demonstrated their boredom by rolling their eyes and sighing loudly. When Jennie asked the children to define the word *kitchen,* they lost patience. The whole class burst into giggles as one of the bolder girls contemptuously replied, "Duh!" Realizing that the lesson was not going well, Jennie became increasingly frustrated. She did not have the experience to evaluate the recommended words in the teacher's guide in terms of the vocabulary knowledge of her students. She simply followed the guidelines for teaching vocabulary and wasted valuable instructional time.

Another day, I was visiting the classroom of Sandi, a veteran second-grade teacher in a very low-performing school that has a lot of English language learners. She was also frustrated with the guidelines in her teacher's guide. "Just look at these words," she complained to me, pointing to the word *grotesque.* "These kids barely speak English, and we're expected to teach them words I did not learn until at least middle school. I'm just overwhelmed and the kids are miserable. I don't feel like we're getting anywhere." Unlike Jennie's basal teacher's guide, which had simplistic vocabulary lists, Sandi's reading anthology included so many difficult words that vocabulary instruction foundered and the children were unable to understand the stories at all.

Jennie and Sandi are typical of many classroom teachers, frustrated with text selections and recommended vocabulary lists. The instructional guidelines they are expected to follow do not work well, particularly with children on opposite ends of the achievement spectrum. These stories underscore an important point: Teachers, not textbook publishers, are most qualified to choose the words that their students need to know.

Teachers know that children need to learn a vast number of words in order to read proficiently but may not be sure which words they should teach. Vocabulary experts suggest that teachers sort words into three tiers based on the frequency and utility of the words (Beck et al., 2002). These categories provide teachers with guidelines for making instructional decisions. Teachers do not need to teach common words categorized as Tier One because most children already know them. Teachers should focus their instruction on Tier Two words, which are high utility and are not already known by most children. Tier Three words are so esoteric or infrequent at a particular grade level that it makes little sense to teach them at all. The word *grotesque,* included in Sandi's second-grade basal reader, is a good example of a Tier Three word.

There is little consensus as to the particular words that belong in the Tier Two category. Each group of children is different in terms of age, preexisting vocabulary, and background knowledge. Experts agree that Tier Two words support comprehension of texts the children are reading and are worth the investment of instructional time because they are likely to be encountered again in other contexts (Beck et al., 2002).

Teachers do not have to depend on textbooks to supply vocabulary lists. Tier Two words are everywhere! Rich, meaningful vocabulary words that children do not already know can be found in the textbooks and trade books that are used for instruction and in books that teachers read aloud to their classes. For example, a fourth-grade teacher might identify the words *concealed, intruders,* and *thrust* from the first chapter of the novel *Island of the Blue Dolphins* (O'Dell, 1960). These words can be categorized in Tier Two because many fourth-grade children do not know them and the words are likely to be encountered again in the books that the children read. The words *pluralism, ethnic,* and *diversity,* found in the first chapter of the fifth-grade social studies book *America Will Be* (Armento et al., 1991), are appropriate Tier Two choices for fifth-grade vocabulary instruction. These words must be taught because they are essential for comprehension of the chapter and are used multiple times in the textbook. The first chapter of the *America Will Be* also contains a number of low-frequency words such as *gumbo, jambalaya,* and *zydeco.* These can be categorized in Tier Three because they are not needed to comprehend the text and are rarely encountered in fifth-grade books. When children encounter Tier Three words in their textbooks, teachers should simply explain what the words mean and move on to more important vocabulary instruction.

EXPLICIT VOCABULARY INSTRUCTION

After identifying the words that children need to learn, teachers must plan vocabulary instruction that will positively affect reading comprehension. Superficial word-learning activities will not suffice. Vocabulary experts have found that effective instruction requires a great deal of time; up to 17 minutes per word is necessary to provide thorough word learning (Beck et al., 2002; Stahl, 1989). The instructional activities included in this chapter are designed to build in-depth word knowledge that promotes reading comprehension.

EVALUATING VOCABULARY DEMANDS OF TEXTS

It is important that the teacher evaluate the vocabulary demands of the text before planning vocabulary instruction. This helps her determine the level of support that the students will need for successful reading.

The teacher copies the text passage that the students will be reading. She underlines the words that might be difficult for her students to understand. Then the teacher evaluates the words based on the guidelines shown in Table 7.1 on page 101.

Conceptual Load

The first aspect of text that is evaluated is conceptual load. Several factors contribute to the conceptual load of a particular word, including the level of abstraction and the background knowledge that children need to make sense of the word. The conceptual load of a particular word varies considerably depending on a particular child's home, community, socioeconomic status, ethnicity, and other factors. For example, the word *blizzard* is concrete and easy to understand for a child who lives in a cold winter climate. The same word might be significantly more difficult for a child who lives in a desert or tropical climate, due to lack of background knowledge. Words that are highly abstract such as *eventually* tend to be conceptually difficult for most children.

Word Utility

Word utility refers to the usefulness of a word. Words that appear frequently in grade-level texts have a high level of utility and are important for children to know. Words that children are unlikely to ever encounter again have a very low level of utility and are probably not worth teaching. This can be a tricky category, because words that appear frequently in texts are often the same words that children already know. Teachers should evaluate words carefully in regard to this topic, in order to identify high-utility words that children do not already know.

Word Frequency

Word frequency refers to the number of times a particular word appears in the text. (A text is defined as an article or a chapter in a textbook or novel.) The word may appear in the same form or in slightly different forms. For example, a text with the words *establish, established,* and *establishment* has three words from the *establish* word family. Children reading this text would encounter the word family *establish* three times, which is a high level of word frequency. This topic is important because repeated exposures is one of the primary ways that children acquire new vocabulary. Texts with high word-frequency levels are likely to support vocabulary acquisition.

Contextual Support

Contextual support measures the degree to which children can infer word meaning from a text. Texts differ in terms of the support they provide in reference to word meaning. The closer the definitional information is to the target word, the easier it is for children to infer word meaning. Contextual support should be carefully evaluated because it is not always helpful and may even be misleading. A text with a high level of contextual support helps children derive word meaning as they read, another important method of vocabulary acquisition. It is important to distinguish texts with a high level of contextual support from those that provide explicit definitions for challenging words. These texts are too considerate and may undermine children's ability to infer word meaning from natural contextual clues in textbooks and novels.

Morphological Support

Morphological support measures the extent to which children can use morphology (examination of word parts) to infer word meaning. High morphological support is often provided by compound words such as *downsize* or by words with high-frequency prefixes or suffixes such as *pre-* or *-tion*. Texts that provide high levels of morphological support encourage children to grapple with word meaning, increasing vocabulary development.

Total Average Score

The total average score is calculated across topics for all underlined words. This score, calculated with a particular group of children in mind, helps the teacher determine whether the vocabulary demands of the text are at an independent (easy), an instructional (moderate), or a frustration (difficult) level for the children.

Percentage of Unknown Words in the Text

The percentage of unknown words in a text passage is determined by dividing the number of unknown (underlined) words by the total number of words. This percentage is not an absolute number because individual children differ in their word knowledge and may have partial or full understanding of the words the teacher has selected. An estimate of the percentage of unknown words helps the teacher determine the amount of vocabulary instruction that children will need in order to understand the text. Researchers agree that children must know 85%–90% of the words in a text in order to read with full comprehension (Freebody & Anderson, 1983; Nagy & Scott, 2000; Stahl, 1989).

Table 7.1.   Rubric for evaluating the vocabulary demands of text.

Vocabulary demand category	Level of demand		
	1 Independent	2 Instructional	3 Frustration
Conceptual load	Words are concrete and label things that most children know about and understand.	Words are somewhat concrete and refer to things some children do not know about or understand.	Words are abstract and represent concepts most children do not know or understand.
Word utility	Words are high utility and are likely to be encountered again in grade-level texts.	Words are of moderate utility and may be encountered again in grade-level texts.	Words are low utility and are unlikely to be encountered again in grade-level texts.
Word frequency	Words are repeated several times in the text, possibly in different forms.	Words appear more than once in the text, possibly in different forms.	Words do not appear more than once in the text.
Contextual support	Contextual support is high.	Contextual support is moderate.	Contextual support is low or misleading.
Morphological support	Word structure provides high level of support.	Word structure provides moderate level of support.	Word structure provides no support.
Percentage of unknown words in the text	A small percentage (less than 10%) of the words in the text are unknown.	A moderate percentage (10%–15%) of the words in the text are unknown.	A high percentage (more than 15%) of the words in the text are unknown.

Example Evaluation of Vocabulary Demands of a Text

Ms. Reed, a fifth-grade teacher, evaluated the vocabulary demand of "Life of a Cowboy" (Schlissel, 1995), prior to beginning instruction. She underlined 10 words in the text she felt were likely to be difficult for the students:

> Crossing open land almost always meant <u>emergencies</u>. A river at flood time could <u>overturn</u> wagons. A drowning, <u>panic-stricken</u> calf might kill the cowboy trying to save it. Flat <u>stretches</u> of land <u>concealed</u> rock and holes that could trip even a <u>sure-footed</u> horse. The bite of a rattlesnake could <u>penetrate</u> a cowboy's boot. Then his only chance would be to cut the flesh between the fang marks and suck out the <u>venom</u>. Some cowboys poured gunpowder on the <u>wound</u> to <u>counteract</u> the poison. (Schlissel, 1995, p. 28)

Then, Ms. Reed evaluated the conceptual load, word utility, word frequency, contextual support, and morphological support for each word based on the rubric (see Figure 7.1).

Evaluating the Vocabulary Demands of a Text

Text: The Life of a Cowboy

Author: Schlissel (1995)

Vocabulary demand category	emergencies	overturn	panic-stricken	stretches	concealed	sure-footed	penetrate	venom	wound	counteract	Average score
Conceptual load	1	1	1	2	2	1	2	1	1	3	1.5
Word utility	1	1	1	2	2	2	2	1	1	2	1.5
Word frequency	2	2	2	2	2	3	2	2	1	3	2.1
Contextual support	2	1	1	1	2	1	1	1	1	2	1.3
Morphological support	3	1	1	3	3	1	3	3	3	1	2.2

Total average score: 1.72

Percentage of unknown words in the text: 12%

Figure 7.1. Evaluating the vocabulary demands of "The Life of a Cowboy" (Schlissel, 1995).

The teacher's analysis of the vocabulary demands of "The Life of a Cowboy" revealed the following information: The percentage of unknown words was 12%, a challenging but appropriate level of difficulty for an instructional text. The total average score was 1.72, indicating that the text was at an easy instructional level for this class. The teacher concluded that the majority of the children in the class would be

Evaluating the Vocabulary Demands of a Text

able to comprehend the text with appropriate instruction. You can use the blank form on page 109 to evaluate the vocabulary demands of a text you are planning to use for instructional purposes.

INSTRUCTIONAL METHODS

Word Study Journal

As important as it is for teachers to select appropriate vocabulary words to teach, it is equally important for children to choose the words they want to learn. The Word Study Journal activity provides children with an individual record of word-learning activities. The purpose is to increase motivation for word learning by providing children with individual choice. The Word Study Journal activity also enhances vocabulary acquisition by providing multiple exposures to new words encountered during reading.

The Word Study Journal includes two components: a transparency master (see p. 110) and a student copy of the Word Study

WORD STUDY JOURNAL

Journal (p. 111). Teachers use the overhead transparency to carefully model recording information in the Word Study Journal. Once the children understand the process, they can use their Word Study Journals to keep a record of their word learning.

In the following vignette, fifth-grade teacher Mr. Hamilton models entering the word *reform* in the Word Study Journal (see p. 110). He demonstrates each step of the process on the overhead transparency, modeling *thinking aloud* to help the children understand his reasoning.

Mr. Hamilton's Class

"Let's see....I need to decide which of the words in this paragraph I should put in my Word Study Journal. I'm not sure what the word *reform* means, so I'll write it in the first box. It says that I also need to write down where the word appeared. So, I'll write that I found it in the social studies book, along with the sentence it appears in: *The colonists understood the importance of political reform.* Now I'm going to try to remember if I heard the word before. I think I remember hearing people talk about it when we had the election. So, I'll write *election* in the MEMORY box. Next, I need to write down the CONTENT AND STRUCTURE strategies I used. I

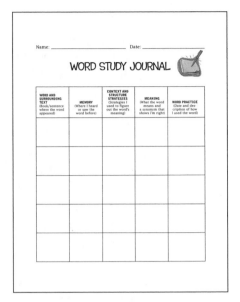

think I can use Study the Structure. I know the word parts *re-* and *form. Re* means *to do something again,* and *form* means *shape or structure.* Now, I can write *Study the Structure* in the CONTEXT AND STRUCTURE STRATEGIES box. Next, I have to write down what I think the word means in the next box. I think *reform* is to change or make something better. So, I'll write that in the MEANING box. I also have to explain why I know I'm right. I'm pretty sure I'm right because Substitute a Synonym works: *The colonists understood the importance of political change.* So, I'll also record that in this box.

The last thing I have to do is tell when and how I used the word. Okay! *(Saturday) I asked my parents to <u>reform</u> the system of chores and allowance in our family.* I'll write it in the WORD PRACTICE box and that's it! I'm finished with the word *reform.*"

The Word Study Journal activity offers children choice in the words that they attend to, a factor that has been shown to increase motivation to learn (see, e.g., Guthrie & Humenick, 2003). Once children have recorded words in their journal, the teacher encourages them to document use of the clarifying strategies—Mine Your Memory, Study the Structure, Consider the Context, and Substitute a Synonym. In addition, Word Study Journals require students to become actively engaged in word learning as they use new words in playful and informal ways.

Mental Imagery

Teachers incorporate the Mental Imagery strategy into word-learning instruction by teaching children to construct a picture of words in their minds in response to the reading of a high-interest text. The purpose of the activity is to stimulate children's imaginations and to help them develop enthusiasm for word learning. Teaching children to construct mental images is not as easy as it sounds, despite the enormous amounts of time many children spend watching visual images on television. When children view visual images, they are engaged in a passive process that is entirely different than the construction of their own mental imagery.

Children were not always passive recipients of visual images. For example, an elderly friend and I were discussing the difference between listening to children's radio and watching children's television. He explained, "When my children were young, they listened to cowboy shows on the radio. When it was time for their favorite show, my boys put on their cowboy hats and guns and grabbed their hobby horses. They were part of the story, riding their horses and shooting their toy guns right along with their favorite characters. Sometimes they jumped out of their seats and wrestled with each other, like the actors on the radio. By the time the show was over, they were worn out and ready for dinner.

"When my great grandchildren watch TV, it's completely different. They just sit there, as if in a trance, and don't move for hours at a time. They even watch the commercials without moving a muscle. When it's time for dinner, they whine and fuss about turning off the TV."

My friend's description of his children's response to radio programming demonstrates an important point. When children create their own mental images, they must draw on prior knowledge and imagination to construct word meaning. All children are capable of constructing mental imagery, but their ability to generate visual images may have been stunted by years of passive exposure to television and video games. They need instruction that will help them recover the ability to generate visual images, which is a powerful word-learning tool.

The vignette in the introduction to this book demonstrates the effectiveness of using vividly written poems to stimulate children's imagination and ability to construct visual images. The teacher asks the children to close their eyes and paint a picture with words in their minds. As the children read the words of the poem, they spontaneously implement strategies needed to infer word meaning. They demonstrate their comprehension with pastel drawings of the mental images they have constructed. The Mental Imagery strategy is an important component of word learning that is particularly effective in developing children's expressive language.

Expressive Vocabulary Cloze

Cloze passages are short texts with missing words. Children fill in the blanks with words that fit the meaning of the text. The purpose of cloze activities is to sensitize children to the nuances of word meaning and to help them develop control

over expressive vocabulary. Cloze activities can be creative and provide a good segue to independent descriptive writing.

Teachers prepare cloze passages by writing short stories with key words that convey meaning. The key words are replaced with blank spaces. Because this kind of cloze activity focuses on developing children's expressive vocabulary, no word bank should be provided with the cloze passage. The children learn to fill in the blanks, altering the story through their vocabulary selections. The Expressive Vocabulary Cloze form on page 112 shows an example of a simple cloze passage suitable for use with younger children or upper-grade students who are in the initial stages of instruction. The teacher gives each table group a different label (e.g., angry, beautiful, young, old, friendly) that the children must use to guide their selection of words for the cloze passage. For example, here is how one group of third graders filled in the cloze passage from the form on page 112. The children's teacher had given them the label *angry* to use to guide their word selections.

> Yesterday we went to the zoo to see the animals. My favorite animal was the angry bear. When I first saw him, he was snarling in the cage. He had sharp teeth. His fur was spiky, and his face was scary. I wanted to get closer. Suddenly the bear attacked. All of the kids were frightened. But I was brave. I can't wait to go back to the zoo to see the angry bear again.

Cloze passages take children beyond inferring word meaning in texts, to expressive word knowledge. Children must have complete control of semantic and syntactic aspects of vocabulary in order to complete this activity. For example, one sentence in the form on page 112 states, *All of the kids were* _____ *But I was* _____. Children must be sensitive to the oppositional meaning that results from the signal word *but* if they are to select appropriate words for the cloze passage.

Getting Into Words with Poetry

Children learn vocabulary more readily when there is a discernible purpose for word learning. Good writing requires words that are rich and interesting. When children are motivated to write well, they often search for the words they need to express themselves, as the vignette about Alex demonstrates (see Introduction). Teachers can accelerate children's vocabulary development through writing activities.

Most children enjoy writing poetry, particularly if they are not required to use a rigid format. Once they are engaged in writing poems, children become highly motivated to capture their thoughts in words. They wrestle with words, struggling to express themselves fluently and thoughtfully. The purpose of writing poetry in vocabulary instruction is to teach children to savor perfectly chosen words.

Getting into words with poetry leads into getting into words with prose. Children become attuned to the nuances of word meaning and the importance of choosing words carefully to express their thoughts. Poetry writing also helps children develop an ear for the sound of words. Gradually, students learn that good writing entails varying sentence patterns and using a wide variety of words.

Evaluating the Vocabulary Demands of a Text

Text: _____   Author: _____

Vocabulary demand category							Average score
Conceptual load							
Word utility							
Word frequency							
Contextual support							
Morphological support							

Total average score: _____

Percentage of unknown words in the text: _____

Directions

1. Choose a text passage, approximately 200 words in length. (For best results, evaluate several text passages, using one rubric for each passage.)

2. Underline words that you think will be difficult for the students, and write them in the boxes at the top of this chart.

3. Evaluate each word in each category as 1 (*independent*), 2 (*instructional*), or 3 (*frustration*). Write the scores in the corresponding boxes.

4. Calculate the average scores for each category. Add the scores for each category, and divide by the total number of words you have evaluated. Record these average scores in the far-right column.

5. Calculate the total average score. Add the average scores for each category, and divide by the number of categories (5). This total average score will tell you whether the text is in the independent, instructional, or frustration range for your students.

6. Calculate the percentage of unknown words in the text by dividing the number of difficult words you have identified by the total number of running words in the passage. (A text with 10%–15% unknown words is appropriate for instruction).

Getting Into Words: Vocabulary Instruction that Strengthens Comprehension by Shira Lubliner (with Linda Smetana)
Copyright © 2005 Paul H. Brookes Publishing Co.

WORD STUDY JOURNAL

WORD AND SURROUNDING TEXT (Book/sentence where the word appeared)	MEMORY (Where I heard or saw the word before)	CONTEXT AND STRUCTURE STRATEGIES (Strategies I used to figure out the word's meaning)	MEANING (What the word means and a synonym that shows I'm right)	WORD PRACTICE (Date and description of how I used the word)
reform Social studies book: "The colonists understood the importance of political reform."	I heard it on the news when they were talking about the election.	I used Study the Structure to figure it out: Re means to do again, and form means to shape. So reform is to shape again or change.	It means to change or make something better. I know I'm right because I used Substitute a Synonym: "The colonists understood the importance of political changes."	(Saturday) I asked my parents to reform the system of chores and allowance in our family.

Getting Into Words: Vocabulary Instruction that Strengthens Comprehension
by Shira Lubliner (with Linda Smetana)

Name: _____ Date: _____

WORD STUDY JOURNAL

WORD AND SURROUNDING TEXT (Book/sentence where the word appeared)	MEMORY (Where I heard or saw the word before)	CONTEXT AND STRUCTURE STRATEGIES (Strategies I used to figure out the word's meaning)	MEANING (What the word means and a synonym that shows I'm right)	WORD PRACTICE (Date and description of how I used the word)

Name: _____ Date: _____

EXPRESSIVE VOCABULARY CLOZE
The Bear

What kind of a bear do you have? (Look at your group's label.) Think about words that describe your bear. Use the words to fill in the blanks in the story.

Yesterday we went to the zoo to see the animals. My favorite animal was the _____ bear. When I first saw him, he was _____ in the _____. He had _____ teeth. His fur was _____, and his _____ was _____. I wanted to get closer. Suddenly the bear _____. All of the kids were _____. But I was _____. I can't wait to go back to the zoo to see the _____ bear again.

Share your bear story with the class. Draw a picture of your bear in the box below.

Getting Into Words: Vocabulary Instruction that Strengthens Comprehension
by Shira Lubliner (with Linda Smetana)

Chapter 8

Graphic Organizers and Word Sorts

Graphic organizers are part of the Tools of Success because they help make thinking visible. Children examine the relationships between words and concepts, relate concepts to prior knowledge, and create graphic representations of their thinking. When children organize information graphically, they are likely to retain word meaning. According to vocabulary research, graphic organizers such as semantic maps, semantic feature analysis charts, and linear arrays are effective methods of developing in-depth word knowledge that supports reading comprehension (Nagy, 1985).

SEMANTIC MAPS

Semantic maps, also called word webs, look like the spokes of a wheel. An important text concept is placed at the center of the map, and lines radiating outward connect the center to related words. The purpose of semantic mapping is to help children identify associations between words. The graphic component in semantic mapping makes it an effective word-building activity, particularly for struggling readers.

Upper-grade teachers can use simple texts such as picture books for initial instruction, moving to more complex texts once the children have mastered word association tasks. For example, one fourth-grade teacher used the picture book *Strega Nona* (de Paola, 1975) to teach children how to construct a semantic map (see Figure 8.1). The topic word, *cooking*, is placed in the center of the semantic map. This word is linked to words found in the book that have to do with cooking.

Once the children are familiar with semantic maps, the teacher can begin using grade-level texts. The following is an example of a fourth-grade semantic mapping activity based on the book *Island of the Blue Dolphins* (O'Dell, 1960). The teacher has selected as a topic words that describe a location for this activity. The first map that the children construct simply lists some of the words mentioned in the first several chapters of the book that relate the word *location* (e.g., *cliff, beach, ledge, shore, cove, cave*).

The teacher increases the complexity of the semantic map by asking the children to think of ways to sort the locations on the island. The children come up with two categories, *high places* and *places by the ocean*. They construct a semantic

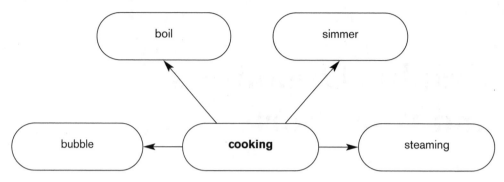

Figure 8.1. Semantic map: *Strega Nona.* (*Source:* de Paola, 1975.)

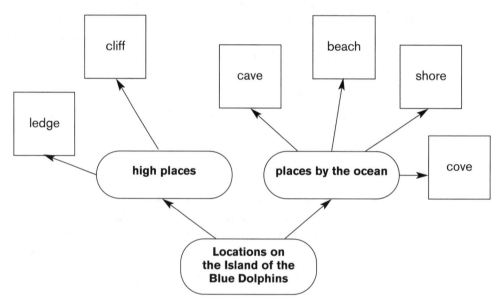

Figure 8.2. Semantic map: *Island of the Blue Dolphins.* (*Source:* O'Dell, 1960.)

map composed of two categories and sort the location words into the appropriate categories (see Figure 8.2). This activity helps the children build connections between groups of semantically related words.

Semantic maps become increasingly valuable as children grow older and are confronted with more challenging vocabulary and unfamiliar concepts in textbooks and novels. Semantic mapping can be used effectively well into high school, helping students organize their thinking about important words and concepts.

SEMANTIC FEATURE ANALYSIS

Semantic feature analysis is a method of vocabulary development based on a matrix. The purpose of feature analysis is to teach the deep meaning of important words associated with a topic. Feature analysis is an effective way to teach the vocabulary and the underlying concepts that are important in understanding a text.

For example, a third-grade class is about to read an article about reptiles. The teacher has created a semantic feature analysis matrix listing various types of reptiles that are discussed in the article, including dinosaurs, snakes, and lizards (see p. 125). Vocabulary words that are found in the text are listed across the top of the matrix. The students read the text and try to discover which words are associated with each type of reptile. The appropriate words are checked off on the matrix as they are encountered in the text. (The first row is completed as an example.) The activity provides the students with repeated exposure to important vocabulary words and a review of the content of the article.

When the children have completed the semantic feature analysis chart, the teacher asks them to choose two reptiles to compare. The following composition, written by third graders Rebecca and David, compares the characteristics of the brontosaurus and tyrannosaurus. Notice how the children have incorporated the new vocabulary words into their writing:

> *We compared two reptiles that were dinosaurs. Both of them were enormous. That means <u>really big</u>. The brontosaurus was vegetarian, so he wasn't really that dangerous. The tyrannosaurus was a carnivore. That means he would eat you if he could because he liked meat. The brontosaurus was sort of dangerous, too. Because he*

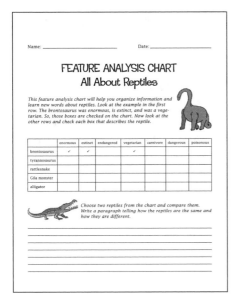

Name: _____   Date: _____

FEATURE ANALYSIS CHART
In the Year of the Boar
and Jackie Robinson

*This feature analysis chart will help you organize information and learn words from the book **In the Year of the Boar and Jackie Robinson**, by Bette Bao Lord. Each word that describes Shirley is checked (first row). Fill out the chart, checking the words that describe Mabel and Emily. Then fill in the chart, checking the words that describe you!*

	humiliated	formidable	obedient	progressive	brainy	ambassador	puny	persuasive
Shirley	✓		✓		✓	✓	✓	
Mabel								
Emily								
You								

Once you have filled out the chart, write a paragraph comparing yourself with your favorite character in the book.

_____

_____

_____

_____

_____

_____

was so big he could step on you and you would die. So, it's pretty lucky that they're extinct.

Feature analysis activities can be adapted for use with different age groups and subject areas. Although the activity is often used with social studies and science vocabulary, it works equally well with literature. The form on page 126 demonstrates a semantic feature analysis chart for the fifth-grade novel *In the Year of the Boar and Jackie Robinson* (Lord, 1984). The first column contains the names of important characters in the book, and the horizontal row includes adjectives found in the book that describe some of the characters. Filling in the feature analysis chart after reading provides the children with a review of story content and practice manipulating important vocabulary words.

WORD SCALES

A word scale, also known as a linear array, is a list of adjectives organized by intensity of a particular characteristic. The purpose of a word scale is to teach children to discriminate between words that describe the same thing. Constructing a word scale requires children to carefully evaluate nuances of word meaning, thus helping to build rich descriptive vocabulary.

The completed word scale shown at the top of page 127 is based on the word *mad.* The fourth-grade teacher guides the children through the *mad* word scale. She then guides them through filling in the *bad* word scale at the bottom of page 127 and then asks them to construct their own word scales with other adjectives (see p. 128). Teachers of younger children can begin instruction by reading aloud the book *Alexander and the Terrible, Horrible, No Good, Very Bad Day* (Viorst, 1972), which provides children with rich examples of words to use in the *bad* word scale. This introductory activity is also recommended for English language learners and other children with weak vocabulary development.

WORD PREDICTION

Mr. Crane opened the newspaper and saw a picture of a small town in Kansas that had been ravaged by a severe storm. As he focused on the picture, a series of words flashed through his mind. His first thoughts were *tornado, cyclone,* and *funnel cloud* because they are words used to describe this kind of storm. Then he considered the damage that the storm had probably caused, and the words *disaster, destruction, ravaged,* and *damaged* occurred to him. Although he hadn't read the article yet, Mr. Crane began to imagine the emotions that people were feeling as a result of the storm. The words *terrified, horrified,* and *frightened* entered his mind as he gazed at the picture. Without conscious effort, Mr. Crane utilized background knowledge about tornadoes to anticipate the vocabulary that would be found in a text.

The importance of prior knowledge in reading comprehension has been extensively documented (Hirsch, 2003; Nagy, 1985; Nagy et al., 1986). Student learning is maximized when teachers build and activate background knowledge, providing children with the opportunity to make connections between new information and that which is already known. Background knowledge is equally important at the word level because words represent concepts that must be understood in order for reading comprehension to occur. Picture Prediction and Title Prediction and Sorting are the Tools of Success that teachers use to build background and vocabulary knowledge.

Some teachers think that word prediction is just like preteaching vocabulary. But, the two activities are actually quite different. Conventional methods of preteaching vocabulary typically entail a passive role for children, who must wait for the teacher to identify the hard words, explain word meaning, and interpret the text. Conventional preteaching of vocabulary reduces the need for children to work hard at word learning or reading comprehension. Methods of word prediction (including the Picture Prediction and the Title Prediction and Sorting activities described next), however, turn over responsibility for word learning to the students. Children become actively engaged as they infer text meaning from

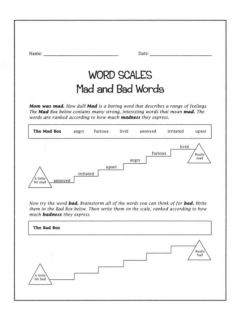

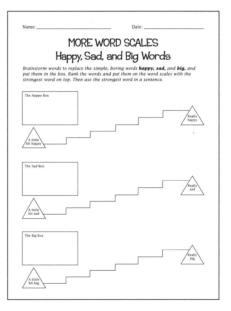

pictures and identify key words associated with the topic. Oral language is the medium for learning, and discussion about the meaning of words builds background knowledge and contributes to vocabulary growth.

Picture Prediction

Picture Prediction is a prereading activity that entails the use of a picture to generate vocabulary words likely to be found in a text. The purpose of Picture Pre-

diction is to provide children with essential vocabulary, background knowledge, and motivation to read a book or text passage. The Picture Prediction activity described in the following vignette is designed for use with younger children. It can also be used effectively in the upper grades to develop picture prediction skills.

Ms. Agnos's Class

Ms. Agnos, a third-grade teacher, knew that many of her students struggled with reading comprehension. Convinced that limited vocabulary contributed to their reading problems, she incorporated vocabulary development activities into reading instruction. Before reading a story about Thanksgiving, Ms. Agnos put a transparency of Picture Prediction: The First Thanksgiving (see p. 129) on the overhead projector. She covered the story on the transparency with a sheet of paper.

Ms. Agnos asked, "Boys and girls, what do you think the story will be about?" The children predicted that the story would be about Thanksgiving. Then she asked, "Which words do you think the author will use to tell this story?" The children began with words that named things found in the picture, such as *Indian, Native American, corn, turkey,* and so forth. Next she asked the children to explain the reason for their predictions and recorded each word and the children's predictions on the chart.

Greg suggested the word *Pilgrim* and explained, "The guys in the black clothes and big hats were Pilgrims. They came here for Thanksgiving."

Name: _____   Date: _____

PICTURE PREDICTION
The First Thanksgiving

Pictures give us clues about a story. They help us think about important words that the author will use to tell the story. Look at the picture below. What important words do you predict will be in the story? How can you tell—what is the reason for your prediction?

Words I predict I'll find	The reason for my prediction

Read the story below. Circle the words that you predicted would be in the story.

In the year 1620 the Pilgrims sailed on the Mayflower. They had planned to arrive in Virginia, but they landed in Massachusetts instead. It was a difficult journey to the new place the Pilgrims called Plymouth Colony.

It was icy cold in Massachusetts that winter. The Pilgrims did not have enough to eat and were very hungry. They survived the first winter thanks to the Wampanoag Indians. The Pilgrims and the Wampanoag signed a peace treaty and promised to be friends. The Native Americans brought the settlers warm blankets and gifts of food, including corn and wild turkey. The Pilgrims celebrated their survival with the holiday of Thanksgiving.

Check to see how many of the words you predicted are in the text. What important words would you add to your list? Write the words in the chart below and explain why they are important.

More important words	Why these word are important

Other children, familiar with the Thanksgiving story, commented on Greg's explanation. "They didn't just come for Thanksgiving. They came here to be free," stated Tiana emphatically.

"When they were free, the Indians made them dinner and then they had Thanksgiving," added Corey.

Ms. Agnos asked if there were other words that should be added to the chart. When the children ran out of ideas, she provided prompts to encourage them to think of additional words. For example, after reminding the children that the Pilgrims landed in Massachusetts by mistake, she asked, "What was the weather like in Massachusetts in the winter?" The children responded with words such as *cold, snowy, icy,* and so forth. Ms. Agnos added their words to the chart and recorded the children's reasoning. Then she told the children that the Pilgrims didn't have time to grow crops before the winter began. She asked, "What do you think happened to the Pilgrims when winter came?" The children responded that they must have been hungry, maybe even starving because they didn't have enough food to eat. Ms. Agnos recorded the words *hungry* and *starving* and the explanations the children gave for their word predictions.

When she felt that the children had predicted most of the story's key vocabulary, Ms. Agnos uncovered the Thanksgiving story and read it aloud while the children followed along. She asked the children to raise their hands each time she read a word on the prediction chart. Ms. Agnos circled these words in the story on the transparency and continued reading. When the class finished reading, Ms. Agnos asked the children if they had overlooked any important words in the story when filling out the prediction chart. The children suggested adding words such as *survived* and *celebrated* to the chart. Ms. Agnos led a discussion as to why these additional words were important in conveying the meaning of the story. She recorded the words and the children's explanations on the chart of more important words on the transparency.

Ms. Agnos used the Picture Prediction strategy to provide her third graders with the vocabulary knowledge they needed to support comprehension of the story. The activity was of particular benefit to the English language learners in the class, providing them with access to key vocabulary and essential background information about Thanksgiving.

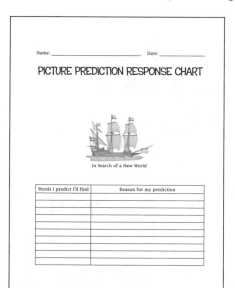

Picture Prediction is particularly useful in preparing children to comprehend challenging texts, as the following activity demonstrates. The picture in this activity is used to help students create a Picture Prediction Response Chart before they read a fifth-grade social studies chapter on explorers.

The teacher guides the students as they make predictions, prompting them if key vocabulary is not spontaneously generated. The following vignette shows the use of a Picture Prediction Response Chart (see p. 130).

Ms. Frank's Class

Ms. Frank: Let's take a look at the picture on the overhead transparency (p. 130). Think about the words that might be used to describe this picture. Can you predict the words that the author will use?

Maika: *Explorers?*

Ms. Frank: (Writes Maika's word on the transparency) Good prediction Maika! Why did you choose the word *explorers?*

Maika: Because I think the picture looks like an explorer's ship.

Ms. Frank: Great! (Write the reason for Maika's prediction on the chart.) What else?

Jacob: *Discover.* The explorers might be about to discover some place.

Ms. Frank: Good prediction! (Writes Jacob's word and explanation on the chart) Anything else? (No response from the students.) What did the explorers have to do to steer their ships?

Jessie: Drive?

Ms. Frank: Okay, what else? (No response) Do you remember the word *navigate?* We learned this word in the last chapter. You have to know how to navigate so you can get where you want to go. (Writes the word *navigate* and the explanation on the chart) Now, let's think of some words that have to do with *navigation.*

Jessie: *Trip, journey?*

Ms. Frank: Good ideas! You take a trip or a journey to a new place. I'm sure you know the word *trip* already, so we don't have to list it. *Journey* is a harder word,

so let's put it on the chart. Can you predict any other words the author might use to describe the journey to the New World?

Sharon: *Route.* That's the way you go someplace.

Jeremy: Yeah, like my paper route!

Ms. Frank: Great! That sounds like a word we might find in this text. (Ms. Frank writes the word *route* and the explanation on the chart. Figure 8.3 shows the Picture Prediction Response Chart that Ms. Frank and her students completed.)

When children have completed the Picture Prediction Response Chart, they are ready to read a small segment of text and look for the words that they have listed on the chart.

Ms. Frank's Class

Ms. Frank: I'm going to read the section of the chapter called "Early Exploration," and I want you to follow along in your books. Watch carefully for words that we predicted. When I'm finished reading, we'll make a check on the chart next to each word that we found. (Reads the text)

PICTURE PREDICTION RESPONSE CHART

In Search of a New World

Words I predict I'll find	Reason for my prediction
explorers	The picture looks like an explorer's ship.
discover	The explorers might be about to discover some place.
navigate	You have to know how to navigate to get where you want to go.
journey	You take a journey to find a new place.
route	The route is the way you go someplace.

Figure 8.3. Completed Picture Prediction Response Chart.

Europeans had longed to discover a speedier route to Asia for many generations. They dreamed of conquering new lands, spreading Christianity, and acquiring great wealth and power. By the 1400s the invention of faster ships and better navigational equipment made it possible for the Europeans to travel more quickly and safely than ever before. Across Europe, nations were launching expeditions across the western ocean. Early explorers did not find a faster route to Asia. They lost their way and discovered America instead. (Source: Armento et al., 1991.)

Let's see. The first line has the word *route*, just like we predicted. Let's look at how it's used. The text tells us that it's the way you go to Asia. (Points to the chart) So, it's just exactly like we predicted. Let's check it off on the chart. Do you see any other words that we predicted?

John: Yeah! *Discoveries.* Is *discoveries* the same as *discover?*

Ms. Frank: Good question! They come from the same word family, so they have similar meaning. *Discover* means *to find something* and *discoveries* are the things that have been found. We can check off the word *discover* on the chart.

Shana: Hey, *discovered* is also in this section.

Ms. Frank: You're right! Here's another member of the *discover* family! Do you see any words that are difficult that we have not listed on the chart? Look for words that might be important in understanding this paragraph.

Cody: *Reality.* It looks important.

Susan: That word is easy. It just means *real.* You can see the word inside.

Ms. Frank: Good work, both of you! Cody picked out an important word, and Susan showed us how we can figure out what it means by using Study the Structure (adds the word to the chart).

Ms. Frank guides this initial reading, modeling for the students how to identify a word in the text and check it off on the chart. She points out important words in the text that should be added and asks the children to justify the reasons for including words on the chart. As mentioned previously, the Picture Prediction activity is more effective than simply preteaching vocabulary words because it increases students' active engagement in the learning process. Although student engagement is heightened by the Picture Prediction activity, children rarely generate all of the important words that will be found in a text. Teachers increase the effectiveness of Picture Prediction by adding words to the prediction list and pointing out the relationship of the words to the picture.

Title Prediction and Sorting

Title Prediction and Sorting entails predicting words based on text features and sorting them into appropriate categories. The purpose of Title Prediction and Sorting is to introduce important vocabulary and to help children become familiar with informational text features such as chapter titles, subtitles, and headings.

Figure 8.4 is an example of a Title Prediction and Sorting activity based on a fifth-grade social studies chapter about explorers (Armento et al., 1991). The teacher begins by listing the title, subtitle and chapter headings on the board or on an overhead transparency (Step 1). She creates a blank word sorting chart and

TITLE PREDICTION AND SORTING

Step 1: Identify major headings in "Early Exploration."

Trade
Religion
Wealth
Power

Step 2: Create a blank word sorting chart.

Trade	Religion	Wealth	Power

Step 3: List word predictions.

expedition	route	riches	explorers
conquer	natives	convert	navigation
discover	treasure		

Step 4: Fill in the word sorting chart (before reading).

Trade	Religion	Wealth	Power
expedition route discover explorers navigation	natives	treasure riches	conquer

Step 5: Check and add to the word sorting chart (after reading).

Trade	Religion	Wealth	Power
✓expedition ✓route ✓discovery ✓explorers navigation spices	✓natives convert	✓treasure ✓riches profit	✓conquer colonies

Figure 8.4. Completed Title Prediction and Sorting activity.

inserts the chapter headings into the boxes at the top of the chart (Step 2). The teacher asks the students to brainstorm, predicting words they think will be found in the chapter (Step 3). She helps the students organize the words into the appropriate boxes on the word sorting chart (Step 4).

When the children have completed the chart, the teacher demonstrates how to read the textbook and check the word predictions on the chart. The teacher reads a passage aloud, inviting the children to stop her when she encounters a word on the chart (Step 5). She demonstrates how to check off the words that she finds in the textbook and adds additional important words that were not on the original chart. When the teacher is sure that the children understand the process, she asks them to work in pairs to read the remaining text passages and to complete their own Title Prediction and Sorting charts.

The Title Prediction and Sorting activity is particularly helpful when used before reading demanding informational texts. The predicting component of the activity helps the children anticipate important concepts and vocabulary, thus building background knowledge. The sorting component of the activity helps the children develop in-depth word knowledge that can be transferred from one learning task to another. Teachers use prediction and sorting activities in conjunction with other word learning tools to ensure that children receive rich, multifaceted vocabulary instruction.

Name: _____   Date: _____

FEATURE ANALYSIS CHART
All About Reptiles

This feature analysis chart will help you organize information and learn new words about reptiles. Look at the example in the first row. The brontosaurus was enormous, is extinct, and was a vegetarian. So, those boxes are checked on the chart. Now look at the other rows and check each box that describes the reptile.

	enormous	extinct	endangered	vegetarian	carnivore	dangerous	poisonous
brontosaurus	✓	✓		✓			
tyrannosaurus							
rattlesnake							
Gila monster							
alligator							

Choose two reptiles from the chart and compare them. Write a paragraph telling how the reptiles are the same and how they are different.

_____

_____

_____

_____

_____

_____

_____

Getting Into Words: Vocabulary Instruction that Strengthens Comprehension
by Shira Lubliner (with Linda Smetana)

Name: _____   Date: _____

FEATURE ANALYSIS CHART
In the Year of the Boar
and Jackie Robinson

*This feature analysis chart will help you organize information and learn words from the book **In the Year of the Boar and Jackie Robinson,** by Bette Bao Lord. Each word that describes Shirley is checked (first row). Fill out the chart, checking the words that describe Mabel and Emily. Then fill in the chart, checking the words that describe you!*

	humiliated	formidable	obedient	progressive	brainy	ambassador	puny	persuasive
Shirley	✓		✓		✓	✓	✓	
Mabel								
Emily								
You								

Once you have filled out the chart, write a paragraph comparing yourself with your favorite character in the book.

_____

_____

_____

_____

_____

_____

_____

Name: _____   Date: _____

WORD SCALES
Mad and Bad Words

Mom was mad. *How dull!* **Mad** *is a boring word that describes a range of feelings. The* **Mad** *Box below contains many strong, interesting words that mean* **mad.** *The words are ranked according to how much* **madness** *they express.*

The Mad Box	angry	furious	livid	annoyed	irritated	upset

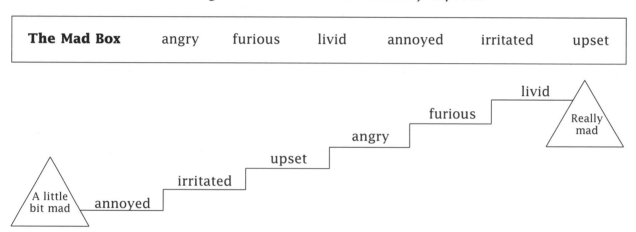

Now try the word **bad.** *Brainstorm all of the words you can think of for* **bad.** *Write them in the Bad Box below. Then write them on the scale, ranked according to how much* **badness** *they express.*

The Bad Box

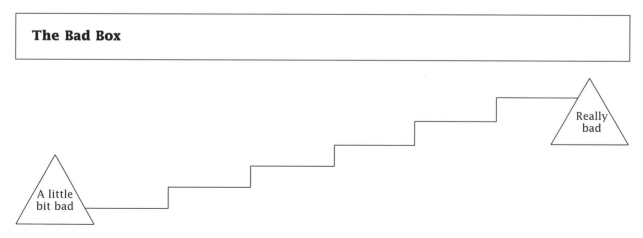

Getting Into Words: Vocabulary Instruction that Strengthens Comprehension
by Shira Lubliner (with Linda Smetana)

Name: _____   Date: _____

MORE WORD SCALES
Happy, Sad, and Big Words

*Brainstorm words to replace the simple, boring words **happy, sad,** and **big,** and put them in the box. Rank the words and put them on the word scales with the strongest word on top. Then use the strongest word in a sentence.*

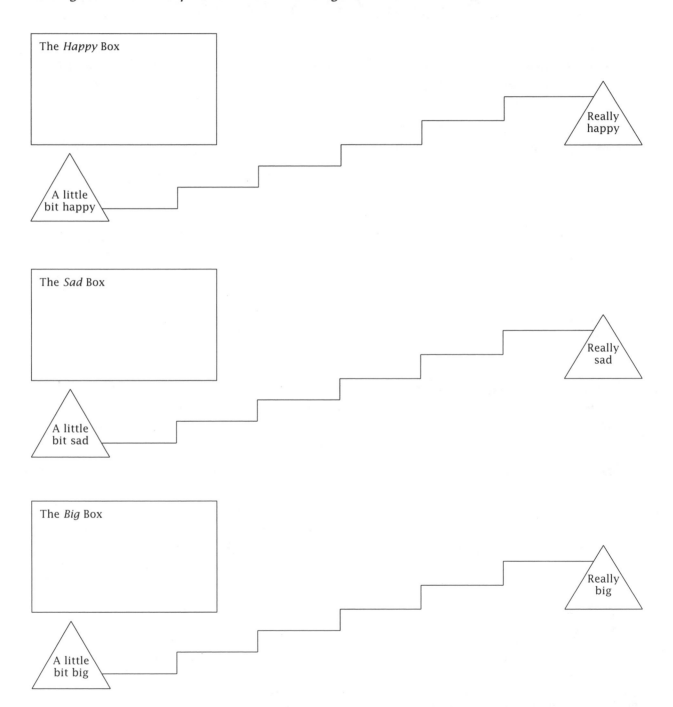

Getting Into Words: Vocabulary Instruction that Strengthens Comprehension
by Shira Lubliner (with Linda Smetana)

Name: _____ Date: _____

PICTURE PREDICTION
The First Thanksgiving

Pictures give us clues about a story. They help us think about important words that the author will use to tell the story. Look at the picture below. What important words do you predict will be in the story? How can you tell—what is the reason for your prediction?

Words I predict I'll find	The reason for my prediction

Read the story below. Circle the words that you predicted would be in the story.

In the year 1620 the Pilgrims sailed on the Mayflower. They had planned to arrive in Virginia, but they landed in Massachusetts instead. It was a difficult journey to the new place the Pilgrims called Plymouth Colony.

It was icy cold in Massachusetts that winter. The Pilgrims did not have enough to eat and were very hungry. They survived the first winter thanks to the Wampanoag Indians. The Pilgrims and the Wampanoag signed a peace treaty and promised to be friends. The Native Americans brought the settlers warm blankets and gifts of food, including corn and wild turkey. The Pilgrims celebrated their survival with the holiday of Thanksgiving.

Check to see how many of the words you predicted are in the text. What important words would you add to your list? Write the words in the chart below and explain why they are important.

More important words	Why these word are important

Getting Into Words: Vocabulary Instruction that Strengthens Comprehension
by Shira Lubliner (with Linda Smetana)
129

Name: _____ Date: _____

PICTURE PREDICTION RESPONSE CHART

In Search of a New World

Words I predict I'll find	Reason for my prediction

Part V

Teaching Vocabulary to Young Children and English Language Learners

Chapter 9

Vocabulary Instruction for Young Children

It was Mother's Day, and my family had gathered for a barbecue. Everyone was watching my 2-year-old twin nephews show off their latest accomplishments. "Gabriel, what's this?" my sister asked, pointing to a picture of a fire hose in the book.

"Ho!" shouted Gabriel gleefully and everyone applauded.

"Daniel, show me the fire engine," my sister asked.

Daniel grinned at his audience and pointed to a picture of a fire engine. The family cheered again. A few minutes later the show ended, and we gathered in small groups to catch up on the latest news. I walked into the living room and observed a charming sight. Daniel and Gabriel were curled up on the couch listening to my daughter Dori read the firehouse book again. Her reading was punctuated with squeals from the twins as they pointed to familiar objects with chubby fingers. It was clear that they had heard the same story dozens of times, which had resulted in a great deal of vocabulary growth and enthusiasm about firehouses.

Scenes like this are so commonplace that few people realize the potent effect they have on children's vocabulary development and ultimate school success. By the time advantaged children such as Daniel and Gabriel enter school, they will know thousands of words more than children from disadvantaged homes (Hart & Risley, 1995, 1999). Some people might shrug and say, "What difference does it make? After all, schools teach children all the vocabulary words they need to know, don't they?"

There is a myth that American schools provide upward mobility and unlimited opportunities to all children. Unfortunately, it is usually not true. Children from disadvantaged families enter school with fewer skills and far less exposure to language and vocabulary than their advantaged classmates (Hart & Risley, 1995, 1999). They lag behind children from more privileged families from the first day of kindergarten and fall further and further behind as they progress through school. School does little to level the playing field for most children from disadvantaged backgrounds (Biemiller, 2004; Chall et al., 1990).

Vocabulary experts agree that teaching disadvantaged children more vocabulary words during the first few years of school is essential if we are to narrow the achievement gap (Biemiller, 2004). The question that educators must answer is

133

how to accelerate children's vocabulary development. Instruction begins with reading aloud to children, a method that simulates the natural vocabulary acquisition of young children such as Daniel and Gabriel.

REPEATED READ-ALOUD

Bedtime stories provide young children with warm memories and rich educational opportunities. The key factors that make this activity so beneficial include exposure to the conventions and language of print, repeated exposures to a wide range of vocabulary words, development of content knowledge that will support future learning, and the strengthening of emotional bonds between young children and their parents. Even when children whose parents have not read to them enter school, it is not too late to capitalize on the benefits of reading aloud. Research has demonstrated that when teachers incorporate repeated oral readings of high-interest children's books into early literacy instruction, disadvantaged children make large gains in vocabulary acquisition (Biemiller, 2004).

A repeated read-aloud program should be carefully structured to maximize children's vocabulary growth. The teacher selects high-interest fiction and nonfiction books with plenty of challenging, high-utility vocabulary words. (For further discussion of high-utility vocabulary words, see Chapter 7.) Instruction begins with a picture prediction activity. The teacher asks the children to look at the cover of the book and predict what it will be about. Prereading discussion focuses on key vocabulary and concepts that may be unfamiliar to the children. (Chapter 8 describes a Picture Prediction strategy for school-age children.)

During the first read-aloud, the teacher does not stop to discuss vocabulary, allowing children to concentrate on global comprehension of the story. She rereads the story several more times during the next few days. During these repeated reading sessions, the teacher stops frequently to discuss challenging words and concepts. She also uses the new words as often as possible in normal classroom discourse. The teacher reads each story at least three times, providing repeated exposures to the new words and increasing the likelihood of vocabulary growth.

Teachers often worry that children will become bored with repeated read-aloud books. Fortunately, however, young children enjoy hearing favorite stories over and over. They enjoy asking questions and pointing out familiar words and illustrations in the text. When children's vocabulary is severely underdeveloped, teachers need to find a variety of ways to increase these children's exposure to repeated story reading. Teachers can recruit volunteers, classroom assistants, or older students to read aloud to young children with weak vocabulary development. Teachers can also increase the benefits of repeated reading by arranging for library visits or creating disposable books to send home with young children. Although parents may not have time to read to their children, older siblings, grandparents, and caregivers often fill in when the family understands that repeated reading of storybooks is expected and beneficial.

As children grow older they continue to benefit from hearing stories read aloud. It is not until middle school that most children's reading comprehension catches up with their oral comprehension. Until that time, children benefit immensely from hearing stories read aloud. When teachers read aloud, they expose children to complex language and vocabulary that children rarely encounter in oral discourse or independent reading.

There is currently a trend toward limiting the range of vocabulary in children's reading books to encourage the development of fluency. Although fluency is important, limiting the number of words that children read may be harmful to their vocabulary development. Without frequent exposure to a wide range of new words, children are unlikely to acquire enough vocabulary to comprehend the textbooks and trade books they will encounter in the upper grades. It is essential that teachers who are using texts with controlled vocabulary provide additional exposure to challenging words by reading aloud to children. Neglecting vocabulary instruction may cause serious long-range problems for children, particularly those who enter school with limited language and vocabulary.

A comprehensive vocabulary development program for young children includes a range of instructional methods. In addition to vocabulary instruction based on repeated read-alouds, teachers help children learn to monitor their own comprehension and provide explicit instruction in word-learning strategies.

WORD-LEARNING STRATEGIES FOR YOUNG CHILDREN

Teachers do not have to wait until children have acquired fluent reading skills to begin clarifying strategy instruction. Even prereaders can learn to use their memory to make sense of unknown words. The following snapshot from the kindergarten classroom of Mr. Lin illustrates this point with a discussion about the children's book *Stellaluna* (Cannon, 1993).

Mr. Lin's Class

Mr. Lin:	Boys and girls, what was Stellaluna like? (The children provide a variety of responses such as *little, sad,* and *lost.*) What were the baby birds like? (The children provide a variety of responses such as *little* and *hungry.*) Do you remember that the author said that the baby birds that Stellaluna met were curious? (The children nod.) That's a tricky word! Now, try to remember! Have you ever heard the word *curious* before?
Tracy:	I know! I know! Curious George!
Several children:	Curious George! Yeah, Curious George, the monkey!
Tommy:	I have a Curious George book. My mom reads it to me.
Mr. Lin:	That's right! A lot of you remember reading stories about Curious George, the monkey. Why did they call him *curious*? (The children ponder the question for a moment.)
James:	Because he was always getting into trouble.
Tommy:	Because he wanted to know about everything.
Lauren:	Because he was curious.
Mr. Lin:	Okay! You've explained why the monkey was called Curious George. Now who can tell me how the baby birds in *Stellaluna* were curious?
Tracy:	They wanted to know how to hang from the nest like Stellaluna, and they could have gotten hurt. Mama Bird got mad at Stellaluna and the baby birds. They got into trouble like Curious George.
Mr. Lin:	That's right! The baby birds in *Stellaluna* were a lot like the monkey Curious George. They wanted to know about everything, and they got into trouble. That's why they're called *curious.*

Many of Mr. Lin's students had partial knowledge of the word *curious.* When he prompted them to remember previous encounters with *curious,* they were able to construct connections with the word as it was used in another, better known text. This allowed them to infer meaning and make sense of the word *curious* in reference to the baby birds in *Stellaluna.* Mr. Lin's instruction provided the children with important modeling that will help them learn to use Mine Your Memory as a clarifying strategy.

First-grade teacher Ms. Morris taught her young students to use structure to figure out word meaning. In the following snapshot, she uses a book about farm ani-

mals to teach the first graders to identify structural clues in compound words. This practice prepares the children for the clarifying strategy Study the Structure.

Ms. Morris's Class

Ms. Morris: Today I'm going to read a story I think you'll enjoy. Look at the picture on the front of the book. Does anyone want to predict what the story will be about?

Eric: It's about cows.

Dina: It's about animals. I see a chicken and a pig and...

Farrah: It's about a farm.

Ms. Morris: You're right! The story is about a farm and the animals that live there. Now I want you to look at this building on the farm. Can anyone guess what the building is called?

Chris: The farmer's house?

Ms. Morris: Yes! It's called a *farmhouse*. You put the words *farm* and *house* together and you get *farmhouse*. Do you see the two little words inside the big word *farmhouse*? (The children nod.) Let's see if you can figure this out. Here is the yard where the animals are playing. It's next to the building where the animals live. Can anyone guess what it's called? (No response)

This building is called a *barn*, right? This is the barn and this is the yard. Now can you figure it out?

Melissa: It's a barnyard!

Ms. Morris: Great, Melissa; you're right! Now follow along in your books as I read the story. (Ms. Morris reads the story, stopping to model clarifying strategies.)

The barn was full of sunlight. Hmm...I wonder what the word *sunlight* means.

Owen: It's light from the sun.

Ms. Morris: That's right! You found the little words hiding inside the big word *sunlight*. Good job! (She returns to the story.)

Young children can begin to identify word parts or use simple context clues with carefully designed strategy instruction. For example, Ms. Morris composed brief texts to introduce the concept of context clues to the children, which will help them later when they learn the clarifying strategy Consider the Context. The following snapshot demonstrates Ms. Morris' instructional methods.

Ms. Morris's Class

Ms. Morris: I'm going to read a part of a story to you. I want you to listen carefully and see if you can figure out what the word *delicious* means. Are you ready? (The children nod.)

Ms. Morris: (Reads aloud) *The food was delicious. The boys liked it so much they ate every bite and asked for more.*
            Now can anyone tell me what *delicious* means?

Matthew: I know! It's good to eat.

Ms. Morris: That's right, Matthew! How did you figure it out?

Matthew: I...I...I just knew it.

Ms. Morris: Let's see if we can help Matthew figure this out. Listen to the story again (rereads the text). Now, does anyone have any idea why Matthew knew *delicious* means *good to eat*?

Melissa: Because they liked it and ate it all up?

Ms. Morris: Good! Matthew and Melissa helped us understand that the story explains exactly what *delicious* means. You are great word detectives!

CLARIFYING CUE CARD FOR KIDS

The following Clarifying Cue Card for Kids (Calling All Word Detectives; see p. 143) is a simplified version of the Clarifying Cue Card (see p. 38) for use with younger children. The Clarifying Cue Card for Kids works well with children in the primary grades and with struggling upper-grade readers. Teachers use the cue card as a scaffold, coaching children to look *at* the word, to look *around* the word, and to look *inside* the word (similar to the clarifying strategies Mine Your Memory, Study the Structure, and Consider the Context, respectively) to figure out word meaning. The final clue, *Think about it!,* is included so that children will consider carefully whether their inference about word meaning makes sense or whether they need to ask for help (akin to the clarifying strategies Ask an Expert and Place a Post-It).

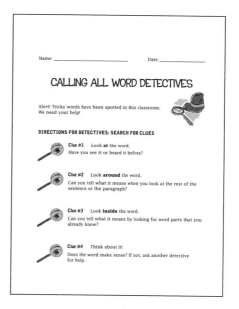

Name: _____   Date: _____

CALLING ALL WORD DETECTIVES

Alert! Tricky words have been spotted in this classroom. We need your help!

DIRECTIONS FOR DETECTIVES: SEARCH FOR CLUES

Clue #1   Look **at** the word.
Have you see it or heard it before?

Clue #2   Look **around** the word.
Can you tell what it means when you look at the rest of the sentence or the paragraph?

Clue #3   Look **inside** the word.
Can you tell what it means by looking for word parts that you already know?

Clue #4   Think about it!
Does the word make sense? If not, ask another detective for help.

The following snapshot took place in a second-grade classroom. The teacher, Mrs. Baker, used a combination of procedural tools (e.g., Clarifying Cue Card for Kids) and conditional tools (e.g., Stop Sign) to help her students make sense of unfamiliar words encountered in the book *The Day the Goose Got Loose* (Lindbergh, 1990).

Mrs. Baker began by reading the text aloud to the children and then handed out a page containing a few lines from the book:

> When the goose got loose she caused a riot.
> Nobody ever thought she'd try it!
> There wasn't any more peace and quiet.
> The day the goose got loose. (Lindbergh, 1990)

Mrs. Baker gave each child a stop sign and explained and modeled the Stop Sign activity (described further in Chapter 2). She pointed to the Clarifying Cue Card for Kids (Calling All Word Detectives; see p. 143) posted on the classroom wall and reminded the children that they would be using clarifying strategies to make sense of words they didn't know.

Mrs. Baker's Class

Mrs. Baker:	Now that we've read the book and talked about it, we're going to be word detectives and look for words we don't understand. Whenever you hear a word you don't know, lift up your stop sign. Then, I'll stop reading and we can talk about the mystery word. First, I'll show you. Watch and see what I do when I come to a hard word. *When the goose got loose she caused a riot.* (She lifts up her stop sign when she reads the word *riot*. The children lift up their stops signs after her.) Hmm...*riot*, that's a hard word. I wonder what it means. Has anyone ever heard this word before?
Mira:	I heard about the riots in the war.
Russell:	Yeah, it was on TV and my dad saw it.
Mrs. Baker:	You're right! There were riots during the war in Iraq. Do you think that riots are a good thing?
Children:	No!
Wali:	My mom said it's bad to mess up things and stuff.
Mrs. Baker:	Okay, so a *riot* causes a lot of trouble. (Points to the Clarifying Cue Card for Kids poster on the wall) Can anyone tell me which clue we used to clarify the word *riot*?
Miguel:	Clue #1?
Mrs. Baker:	Right! Clue #1 reminds us to look *at* the word, to see if we've seen it or heard it before. You did a great job of remembering the word *riot*. (Returns to text) Do you think people were happy when the goose caused a *riot*?
Children:	No!
Mrs. Baker:	Now, I'm going to continue reading. It's your turn to listen for tricky words and to hold up your stop signs. Do you think you can do it? (The children nod enthusiastically.) Okay, let's get started. *Nobody ever thought she'd try it! There wasn't any more peace....* (Stop signs go up when Mrs. Baker reads the word *peace*.)

> Good work, word detectives! You found a very hard word! Let's see if we can figure it out. Try Clue #1: Look *at* the word. Has anyone seen or heard this word before?

Stephanie: I've heard it before. My mom is always saying she wants some peace and quiet. She doesn't like it when my brother and me fight and make a lot of noise.

Brian: Peace is like not fighting.

Mrs. Baker: Great! You've got it! *Peace* is when everyone gets along and we don't hear sounds of fighting. (Returns to text) Hmm... So, when the book says there was a riot and there wasn't any more *peace* and *quiet,* we can tell that the goose caused a lot of trouble.

> Now, here a hard question: Which clues did we use this time?

Sara: The first one; I remembered what my mom said.

Mrs. Baker: Right, Sara did a good job of remembering that she heard the word before. (Points to the poster) Did anyone use any other clues? (No response from the children) How about Clue #2? Did we look at the rest of the words in the sentence, like *quiet* to get an idea of what *peace* means? (Children nod) Good work, word detectives! Let's continue!

At this early stage of instruction, Mrs. Baker focuses on the development of word consciousness, an essential component of word-learning proficiency (Scott & Nagy, 2004). She encourages the children to monitor their comprehension carefully as she reads aloud. When the children raise their stop signs, she initiates a clarifying discussion, thus helping the children construct word meaning. As the children's metacognitive skills develop, Mrs. Baker will focus more attention on the Clarifying Cue Card for Kids, asking the children to identify the strategy that provides the best clues.

The snapshot from Mrs. Baker's classroom demonstrates that Mine Your Memory is a particularly powerful clarifying strategy, typically the first strategy to be independently controlled by young readers. The other clarifying strategies, such as Consider the Context, are more difficult for the children to understand and implement. Although Mrs. Baker's students link the combination of words *peace* and *quiet* in the text, they rely on Mine Your Memory (Sara's recollection of what her mom said) rather than using Consider the Context as a separate strategy. Mrs. Baker reinforces the use of context by returning to the text and pointing out that there was no peace because the goose caused a lot of trouble and, in fact, causes a riot! These second-grade children are demonstrating emerging control of the clarifying strategies, necessary to the development of independent word-learning skills.

Just as older children need a multifaceted approach to vocabulary instruction, young children benefit from an approach that addresses the three dimensions of vocabulary knowledge. Children learn to use clarifying strategies (procedural knowledge) as teachers model the use of the Clarifying Cue Card for Kids. Children learn to monitor their own word learning and to regulate strategy use (conditional knowledge) through instruction based on the Stop Sign for Unknown Words activity. Finally, teachers help children learn words (declarative knowledge) through repeated read-alouds. All of these methods are taught as teachers read aloud high-interest books with a great number of challenging words. Over time this instruction accelerates children's vocabulary acquisition. Children learn up to three words per day from repeated read-alouds (Biemiller, 2004) and develop essential word-learning strategies that will help them become independent word learners as their decoding skills emerge.

Name: _____   Date:_____

CALLING ALL WORD DETECTIVES

Alert! Tricky words have been spotted in this classroom.
We need your help!

DIRECTIONS FOR DETECTIVES: SEARCH FOR CLUES

 Clue #1   Look **at** the word.

Have you see it or heard it before?

 **Clue #2**   Look **around** the word.

Can you tell what it means when you look at the rest of the
sentence or the paragraph?

 Clue #3   Look **inside** the word.

Can you tell what it means by looking for word parts that you
already know?

 **Clue #4**   Think about it!

Does the word make sense? If not, ask another detective
for help.

Chapter 10

Vocabulary Instruction for English Language Learners

It was a bright fall morning when I visited East Park Elementary to observe reading groups for English language learners. The principal suggested that I observe twin sisters Seena and Raya, the least proficient readers in the third grade. She explained that the girls' immigrant parents worked long hours and were rarely available to supervise their homework or to participate in school-related activities. According to the principal, Seena's and Raya's English vocabulary was very limited despite the fact that they had been born in the United States and had attended this school since kindergarten.

The following snapshot took place in Seena's classroom as her teacher Ms. Ruiz conducted a guided reading group for English language learners. The children were reading a leveled text (at an emergent reading level) about barnyard animals. The following snapshot is an excerpt of the reading lesson, focusing on an interchange between Ms. Ruiz and Seena.

Seena's Reading Lesson

Ms. Ruiz: Boys and girls, here's the book we're going to read today. It's called *Barnyard Animals*. Do you remember what we worked on last time? Seena?

Seena: Um...I forget.

Ms. Ruiz: We worked on chunking—reading whole chunks of words that we know. Okay? (Children nod.) Now, Seena, you go first. Start reading on page 1. Remember to look at the pictures if you need a clue.

Seena: (Reads haltingly) *Many animals live in the bar...n...yar...d* (reads the word with an obvious lack of comprehension). *There are ten ch...* (looks at the picture) *chickens. There are ducks, too. The big white g...g...* (Seena stops, unable to read the word *goose*. She checks the picture but can't find a clue for the unfamiliar word.)

Ms. Ruiz: Sound it out. You've got the first letter. Now, what sound do two os make? Remember? (No response) It's a long /u/ sound. So you have the chunk, /gu/... Now, what's the last sound in the word?

Seena: /s/?

Ms. Ruiz: Good! Now put the sounds together. What word does /g/.../u/.../s/ make? (No response) It rhymes with *moose*: /g/.../us/. Can you say it?

Seena: (Without comprehension) /g/.../us/?

Ms. Ruiz: That's it! (Turns the page and points to a picture of a goose) *Goose!*

Seena: Oh, *goose!* I get it! (Turns back to the line on the previous page and reads) *The big white goose was in the barn.*

The effects of vocabulary limitations on Seena's reading performance were evident throughout this lesson. Although she was able to decode most of the phonemes, she did not appear to associate many of the sounds with meaningful words. Ms. Ruiz tried to help but limited her support to graphophonic cues, directing the children to sound out the unfamiliar words. When Seena tried to sound out the word *goose,* she could not check if she had decoded it correctly because she did not recognize the word. Seena's lack of vocabulary knowledge precluded self-monitoring and limited the utility of the graphophonic cues. This resulted in a frustrating and unsuccessful reading experience.

A few minutes later I entered Raya's classroom and found that her teacher, Ms. Valdez, was using the same leveled book in a guided reading lesson with her English language learners. Meeting briefly with me before the lesson, Ms. Valdez explained that she designed instruction to address the vocabulary limitations that complicated the children's efforts to learn to read. She noted that English language learners are often somewhat familiar with common English words but lack the automatic lexical access needed to support reading. In order to address this problem, Ms. Valdez used the Picture Prediction activity to preview vocabulary and to help the children connect the sounds that they decoded with meaningful words.

The following is a snapshot of the reading lesson, focusing on Raya's instruction.

Raya's Reading Lesson

Ms. Valdez: Boys and girls, today we're going to read a book about barnyard animals (shows the children the picture on the cover of the book). Look, here's a picture of a barnyard on the cover of the book. Do you know where we could find a barnyard?

Juana: At a farm?

Ms. Valdez: Right! Now, what kinds of animals live in a barnyard?

Mateo: Cows?

Ms. Valdez: Yes, there are some cows in the picture. (Points to the picture) What other kinds of animals do you see in the barnyard?

Juana: Ducks?

Ms. Valdez: Yes, there's a duck right here! (Turns the page) What other kinds of animals do you see? Raya?

Raya: Turkeys and chickens, and...I don't know.

Ms. Valdez: Look (points to the picture), this bird is bigger than a chicken and smaller than a turkey. Can you remember what it's called? Try Mine Your Memory.

Raya: I can't remember.

Ms. Valdez: Do you remember the book we read called *The Day the Goose Got Loose?*

Raya: Oh yeah! I remember now. Goose!

Ms. Valdez: Good! Now let's look at the pictures and see if we've forgotten anything. What's this? Mateo?

Mateo: The farmer?

Ms. Valdez: Right! What's the machine called that the farmer is sitting on?

Raya: It's a wagon or something. I can't remember.

Ms. Valdez: Try Mine Your Memory. Do you remember seeing this farm machine in a book we read last week?

Raya: Oh yeah! It was a book about a little red tractor!

Ms. Valdez: Great! You remembered that it's a tractor. So, we have a farmer, barnyard, and a tractor, and what kind of the animals are in the barnyard?

Raya: (Points to the picture) A turkey, some chickens, some ducks, a dog, and a cat...

Ms. Valdez: Right, a turkey, chickens, ducks, a dog, a cat, and a what?

Raya: A goose!

Ms. Valdez: Okay, you've got it! Now let's read the book.

The careful preparation that Ms. Valdez provided to the English language learners was effective in supporting their reading. When she previewed the names of the tractor and the barnyard animals, Ms. Valdez provided the children with essential vocabulary and background knowledge that they needed to construct meaning from the book. She provided explicit phonics instruction and guided the children's attempts to decode familiar words. Ms. Valdez taught the children to use the clarifying strategy Mine Your Memory when they struggled with difficult words. This is an important strategy for English language learners to master because they often lack rapid lexical access to partially known words. Using Mine Your Memory helps children such as Raya access word knowledge and apply it to reading tasks. Once she accessed the vocabulary, Raya could use graphophonic cues to monitor her own reading. Vocabulary knowledge was the key to a successful reading experience.

It is also important to note that Ms. Valdez made use of thematically related texts to build word knowledge. She helped the children build associations between words found in a variety of books about farm animals and equipment. The use of thematically related texts offers multiple exposures to high-utility words, an important component of vocabulary acquisition. Books about a common theme also help children acquire background knowledge that they need in order to read proficiently in English.

SPANISH-SPEAKING CHILDREN

Spanish-speaking children are the fastest growing segment of the U.S. school population. According to demographic data, 79% of English language learners in American schools speak Spanish as their first language (Kindler, 2002). Many of these children struggle with difficulties related to learning English, putting them at risk for academic failure. The goal of instruction for Spanish-speaking children is to provide content knowledge and mastery of academic English while preserving ethnic pride and competence in the children's native language.

Spanish-speaking children benefit from carefully designed reading instruction such as that provided by Ms. Valdez in the previous vignette. Helping children

acquire and access key academic vocabulary (the declarative dimension) is one component of instruction. Additional components include instruction in clarifying strategies and metacognitive skills, with an emphasis on the use of cognates. Teachers can encourage pride in children's native culture by exposing the children to great literature and poetry written in Spanish. Once children learn to enjoy poetry in Spanish, they can be encouraged to write their own poetry in both languages. Children are often motivated to learn English vocabulary as they wrestle with the words needed to express the ideas that they want to share with others.

CLARIFYING STRATEGY INSTRUCTION

Teachers can help Spanish-speaking children acquire vocabulary by teaching them to use clarifying strategies. The Clarifying Cue Card with Catch a Cognate is provided in English (see p. 156) and in Spanish for use with Spanish-speaking children (see p. 157). The Study the Structure and Consider the Context Cue Cards are also provided in Spanish (see pp. 158–159).

Clarifying strategy instruction that includes Catch a Cognate is particularly helpful for Spanish-speaking children. Vocabulary experts estimate that more than one third of adult vocabulary in English is composed of cognates (Nash, 1997). In fact, 53.6% of English words have Romance language origins (Hammer, 1979). Children who speak other Romance languages may also benefit from cognate instruction; however, differences in spelling and pronunciation between English and these other languages (e.g., French) may make this strategy difficult for children to implement effectively.

Teaching Spanish-speaking children to recognize and use cognates as a word-learning strategy provides them with access to a broad array of important academic English words. Children need a great deal of modeling and practice in order to Catch a Cognate effectively. The Catch a Cognate Cue Card (in English or in Spanish, see pp. 160–161, respectively) and Catch a Cognate Worksheet (see p. 162) can be used for instruction.

CLARIFYING CUE CARD WITH CATCH A COGNATE

When you find a word you don't understand, try the following strategies:

MINE YOUR MEMORY
Have you ever seen this word before? Can you remember what it means?

STUDY THE STRUCTURE
Do you know the root or base word? Does the word have a prefix or suffix that you know? Try to use clues in the word to figure out the meaning.

CONSIDER THE CONTEXT
Look at the information in the sentence and the whole paragraph. Can you figure out the meaning of the word?

SUBSTITUTE A SYNONYM
When you think you know what the word means, try putting a word with a similar meaning in the sentence. Does it make sense?

If the strategies don't work, try these:

ASK AN EXPERT
Does someone in your group know what the word means? Can you figure it out together?

PLACE A POST-IT
If you can't figure out the meaning of the word, put a Post-It by the word, and check with the teacher or look it up in the dictionary later.

If you speak Spanish, try this:

CATCH A COGNATE
Does the word look or sound like a word you know in Spanish? Try the Spanish word's meaning to see if it makes sense.

TARJETA CON CLAVES PARA CLARIFICAR CON ATRAPE UN COGNADO
(Spanish Translation of Clarifying Cue Card with Catch a Cognate)

Cuando encuentre una palabra que no entiende, use las estratégias siguientes:

USE SU MEMORIA
¿Ha visto esta palabra antes? ¿Recuerda qué significa?

ESTUDIE LA ESTRUCTURA
¿Sabe la raíz o base? ¿La palabra tiene un prefijo o sufijo que conoce? Use claves reconocidas en la palabra para adivinar el significado.

CONSIDERE EL CONTEXTO
Fije en la información en la oración y el párrafo. ¿Puede adivinar el significado?

SUSTITUYA UN SINÓNIMO
Si piensa que sabe el significado de la palabra, trate de poner una palabra con significado parecido en la oración. ¿Tiene sentido?

Si las estratégias no le resultan, trate lo siguiente:

PREGÚNTELE A UN EXPERTO
¿Alguien en su grupo sabrá lo que la palabra significa? Trabajando junto ¿pueden adivinar el significado?

PÓNGALE UN POST-IT
Si no puede adivinar el significado de la palabra, ponga un Post-It junto la palabra y pregúntele a la maestra o busque la palabra en el diccionario.

ATRAPE UN COGNADO
¿La palabra parece o suena como una palabra que conoce en español? Use el significado de la palabra en español para ver si tiene sentido.

The following is a snapshot of a sixth-grade class composed mainly of Spanish-speaking students. Mr. Mitchell is teaching the children how to use the Catch a Cognate strategy.

Mr. Mitchell's Class

Mr. Mitchell: Today we are going to work on cognates. Cognates are words that look or sound alike in two languages, such as Spanish and English, and mean nearly the same thing. There are many Spanish–English cognates in these books (points to a pile of textbooks on his desk). When you learn how to use Catch a Cognate, you will understand a lot of new words in English. So, pay attention! This is really going to help you!

Let's take a look at this Catch a Cognate Cue Card. (Mr. Mitchell hands out copies of the cue card and puts a matching transparency on the overhead projector.) I want you to follow along as I read each step on the cue card (reads the steps from the cue card).

Now, let's try an example. (Mr. Mitchell removes the Catch a Cognate Cue Card transparency, then hands out copies of the Catch a Cognate Worksheet and puts a matching transparency on the overhead projector.) Look at the sentence on the overhead:

Her heart beat rapidly after running to class.

Can anyone help with the first step?

Maria: I look at *rapidly* and think it looks like *rápido en español.*

Mr. Mitchell: Excellent, Maria! That's exactly what you need to do. What does *rápido* mean in English?

Maria: Fast?

CATCH A COGNATE CUE CARD

Cognates are words that look or sound alike in two languages and mean nearly the same thing. There are many Spanish-English cognates. When you learn how to catch cognates, you will understand a lot of new words in English.

When you find an English word you don't understand, follow these steps:

LOOK AND LISTEN
Look at the English word. Does it *look* like a word you know in Spanish? Read it aloud. Does it *sound* like a Spanish word?

CONSIDER IT
Do you know what the word means in Spanish?

TRY IT
Read the whole sentence, using the Spanish word instead of the word in English.

THINK ABOUT IT
Think about it! Does the word make sense in the sentence? If it makes sense it's a cognate!

Celebrate! You've caught a cognate and learned a new word!

TARJETA CON CLAVES: ATRAPE UN COGNADO
(Spanish Translation of Catch a Cognate Cue Card)

Cognados son palabras que parecen y suenan similar en dos idiomas y tienen un significado muy similar. Hay muchos cognados español-inglés. Cuando aprenda a atrapar cognados, va a entender muchas más palabras en inglés.

Cuando vea una palabra en inglés que no entiende, siga los siguientes pasos:

MIRE Y ESCUCHE
Mire la palabra en inglés. ¿Se ve como una palabra que conoce en español? Lea la palabra en voz alta. ¿Suena como una palabra que conoce en español?

CONSIDERE
¿Sabe lo que la palabra significa en español?

INTENTE
Lea la oración completa usando la palabra en español en lugar de la palabra en inglés.

PIENSE
¡Piense! ¿Tiene sentido la palabra en la oración? Si tiene sentido, ¡es un cognado!

¡Celebre! ¡Atrapó un cognado y aprendió una palabra nueva!

Mr. Mitchell: Right! Now, I need someone to try the word in a sentence to make sure it makes sense. Lourdes?

Lourdes: Her heart beat was *rápido* after running to class.

Mr. Mitchell: Good! Do we know for sure that *rapidly* is a cognate? Maria?

Maria: Ah...I don't know.

Mr. Mitchell: Does the word mean more or less the same thing in English and Spanish?

Maria: Yes.

Mr. Mitchell: Good! You're right! *Rapidly* and *rápido* are cognates because they mean the same thing in both languages. Now, I'm going to give you some sentences to work on. Each sentence has an underlined word that might be a cognate. I want you try to figure out if the word is a cognate and what it means. We'll do the first sentence together:

> Sparta had a different <u>system</u> of government than Athens.

Okay, who wants to start? Is the word *system* a cognate?

Antonio: Yeah!

Mr. Mitchell: How do you know?

Antonio: I think it sounds like *sistema* in Spanish.

Mr. Mitchell: Good! Did everyone notice that it's easier to hear how the words *system* and *sistema* are alike than it is to see how they are alike? That's because *system* is written with *y* in English and *sistema* is written with *i* in Spanish. But when you say the words, they sound very similar. Okay, Antonio, now try *sistema* in the sentence. Does it make sense?

Antonio: Yeah, it makes sense! Sparta had a different *sistema del gobierno*.

Mr. Mitchell: Great, Antonio! You figured out that *system* and *government* both have cognates in Spanish.

Mariela: *Diferente* is a cognate, too. The whole sentence is cognates.

Mr. Mitchell: Mariela just pointed out something really important. Cognates are everywhere! In this sentence alone, we found three of them. If you learn to find cognates, you'll understand a lot more English. Does everyone understand how catching cognates helps you understand the sentence?

Name: _____ Date: _____

CATCH A COGNATE WORKSHEET

*Many of the words we use in school are similar in Spanish and English. For example, the word **similar** is exactly the same in both languages. Use the Catch a Cognate Cue Card to help you figure out if an unknown word is a cognate. Here is an example: **Her heart beat rapidly after running to class.***

1. **Look and listen.** Look at the word *rapidly*. Does it look like a word you know in Spanish? Does it *sound* like a Spanish word? Could it be a cognate?
   Rapidly looks and sounds a lot like the word rápido in Spanish.
2. **Consider it.** Do you know what the word means in Spanish?
   The word rápido in Spanish means fast.
3. **Try it.** Read the whole sentence using the Spanish word instead of the word in English.
   Her heart beat was rápido after running to class.
4. **Think about it.** Does the word make sense in a sentence?
   Yes, rápido makes sense in the sentence. I think it's a cognate!

Work with a partner and find each of the English cognates for the Spanish words in parentheses. Follow the steps on the Catch a Cognate Cue Card.

1. The cave paintings were made by prehistoric people. (*prehistórico*)
2. Discuss the characteristics of the people in the New England colonies. (*característicos*)
3. What is the correct abbreviation for the state of California? (*abreviatura*)
4. Find the congruent shapes. (*congruente*)
5. Write the definition of each word. (*definición*)

With your partner, identify cognates for the underlined words using the Catch a Cognate Cue Card.

1. Explain how the <u>system</u> works.
2. <u>Combine</u> these numbers.
3. <u>Describe</u> the character in the story.
4. What does this <u>symbol</u> mean?
5. Give <u>biographical</u> information about yourself.

Write some sentences of your own, using words that are cognates. Give your sentences to a friend and ask him or her to catch your cognates.

_____
_____
_____
_____

Students: Yeah!

Mr. Mitchell: It's really important that you always check to make sure that a cognate makes sense. Sometimes a word is tricky. It looks like a cognate, but it doesn't mean the same thing in Spanish and English. So, be sure to check your work.

Now, I want each of you to work with a partner on the rest of the sentences on your Catch a Cognate Worksheet. Look at the underlined word in each sentence and decide if it's a cognate. Then try to figure out what the word means in Spanish and if it makes sense in English. Any questions? Okay, Let's get started.

While the children work, Mr. Mitchell circulates around the room, offering suggestions and answering questions. The explicit instruction and practice that Mr. Mitchell provides to his Spanish-speaking students teaches them to use important tools for making sense of unfamiliar words they encounter while reading. Following are guidelines for cognate instruction.

COGNATE CLUES FOR TEACHERS

1. Cognates can be very helpful to Spanish-speaking students who are learning English. Methods of identifying cognates and using them for comprehension of English texts must be *explicitly taught.*

2. Teach students to use the Catch a Cognate Cue Card in initial stages of cognate instruction. Model each step of catching cognates, and provide many opportunities for practice. Gradually students will learn to use the Catch a Cognate strategy independently and effectively while reading English texts.

3. Teach students to *look* at the English word and try to think of a *similar-looking* word in Spanish.

4. Teach them to also read the word *aloud* and listen for the *sound* of a *similar word* in Spanish. It is important to teach students to *listen for the sound* of cognates because the words do not always look alike. It can be tricky to recognize cognates in text due to differences in how the words are spelled in English and Spanish. Words spelled with *ph* in English (an /f/ sound) are spelled with *f* in Spanish. For example, *photography* in English is *fotografía* in Spanish. English words that have a short /i/ sound spelled with the letter *y*, such as *symbol*, have Spanish cognates that spell the vowel sound with the letter *i* (*símbolo*). English

words that end with *y*, such as *primary* or *allegory*, often have Spanish cognates ending with *-io* or *-ia* (*primario, alegoría*). Other nouns that end in *y* in English have Spanish cognates that end with *-dad*. For example, *electricity* in English is *electricidad* in Spanish. Adverbs typically end with *-ly* in English and *-mente* in Spanish. For example, *exactly* in English is *exactamente* in Spanish.

5. The purpose of the Catch a Cognate strategy is to help children infer the meaning of English words they encounter while reading. It is not necessary to identify the exact translation of a cognate or the correct part of speech. For example, the word *rápido* sounds similar to *rapidly* and provides the children with word meaning, even though the exact translation of *rapidly* is *rápidamente*.

The Catch a Cognate Worksheet (see p. 162) provides additional Catch a Cognate practice for Spanish-speaking children. The cognates in this activity include vocabulary words that appear frequently in upper elementary and middle school textbooks, such as *prehistoric, definition, combine, describe, symbol,* and *biographical.*

NATIVE LANGUAGE POETRY

Educating English language learners entails more than teaching them English words and word-learning strategies. Children must be motivated to learn so that they will exert the effort necessary for academic success. The inclusion of culturally relevant literature in the language arts curriculum is an important factor in engaging the interest of English language learners. Native language poetry is a particularly important tool in the instruction of English language learners. Teachers can download poems in Spanish and many other languages from the Internet. Poems are often published in the original language accompanied by English translations, allowing all of the children in the class to benefit from instruction. For example, Latino children can be invited to share poetry by renowned Spanish language poets such as Federico García Lorca. Listening to Spanish poetry exposes monolingual English-speaking children to the richness of Hispanic culture, while fostering Latino children's pride in their native culture and language. The following vignette describes Mañuel, a troubled Latino youngster who was inspired by Spanish poetry.

Mañuel's Story

Mañuel and his two brothers lived with their father in a tough, low-income neighborhood. The boys were often in trouble at school, and their father worked long hours and was rarely available to speak to the teachers or principal about his sons' behavioral or learning problems. Mañuel was entering fifth grade with a discipline problem and had been designated as being at risk of academic failure.

The principal placed Mañuel in Mrs. Cohen's class, hoping that the multicultural curriculum she used would motivate Mañuel to take an interest in school. The first day of school did not look promising. Mrs. Cohen welcomed the children to class and noted that Mañuel appeared sullen and withdrawn. Despite her efforts to engage him in learning activities, Mañuel remained uncooperative. He was involved in a fight on the playground later that week and was suspended.

On the day that Mañuel returned, Mrs. Cohen introduced a poetry unit to the children. She passed out a poem written in Spanish and translated into English and invited the children to follow along in the language of their choice. "Those of you who speak Spanish are so lucky," she told the children. "You can read some of the most beautiful poetry ever written. Listen while I read this poem by Federico García Lorca. Even if you read it in English, be sure to pay attention to the sound of the words in Spanish."

The children read poems by García Lorca and Pablo Neruda along with poetry by a wide assortment of English language poets. Mrs. Cohen noticed that Mañuel seemed to perk up whenever she read a poem by a Spanish language poet. One day Mañuel appeared in class, lugging a large book around with him. When Mrs. Cohen inquired about the book, Mañuel proudly explained that he had taken several buses from his home to the public library, where he had checked out a huge anthology of García Lorca's poems (in Spanish). Whenever he had a free moment, Mañuel read the book. He studied the poems and read them aloud to anyone who would listen. The principal, other teachers, the custodian, and the cafeteria workers were all treated to his poetry readings.

Gradually, Mañuel emerged from his brittle shell. He began to show an interest in classroom activities and started writing his own poems. At first he concentrated on writing in Spanish but found a limited audience for his work. Then he began to experiment with English poetry and was pleased with the results. Although Mañuel continued to struggle in many areas of the curriculum, his reading and writing skills soared. He wrestled with words every day, determined to improve the quality of his poems. Mañuel found a purpose for learning in García Lorca's beautiful poetry.

Teachers can motivate children like Mañuel by showing respect for their native culture and encouraging them to model themselves after great Spanish language poets. Incorporating native language poetry can be an effective method of engaging student interest and providing a purpose for vocabulary acquisition.

EFFECTIVE INSTRUCTION FOR ENGLISH LANGUAGE LEARNERS

English language learners are confronted with a huge task. They must learn a vast number of English words while acquiring content knowledge presented in English, a language they do not understand well. English language learners, particularly those in the upper elementary grades and middle school, need multifaceted instruction that accelerates vocabulary acquisition. Effective instruction for English language learners addresses the three dimensions of vocabulary knowledge, providing access to clarifying strategies (procedural knowledge), metacognitive skills (conditional knowledge), and academic English words (declarative knowledge). Spanish-speaking children derive particular benefit from instruction in the use of cognates. In addition, the curriculum must convey to English language learners that their language and culture are valued.

CLARIFYING CUE CARD
WITH CATCH A COGNATE

When you find a word you don't understand, try the following strategies:

MINE YOUR MEMORY

Have you ever seen this word before? Can you remember what it means?

STUDY THE STRUCTURE

Do you know the root or base word? Does the word have a prefix or suffix that you know? Try to use clues in the word to figure out the meaning.

CONSIDER THE CONTEXT

Look at the information in the sentence and the whole paragraph. Can you figure out the meaning of the word?

SUBSTITUTE A SYNONYM

When you think you know what the word means, try putting a word with a similar meaning in the sentence. Does it make sense?

If the strategies don't work, try these:

ASK AN EXPERT

Does someone in your group know what the word means? Can you figure it out together?

PLACE A POST-IT

If you can't figure out the meaning of the word, put a Post-It by the word, and check with the teacher or look it up in the dictionary later.

If you speak Spanish, try this:

CATCH A COGNATE

Does the word look or sound like a word you know in Spanish? Try the Spanish word's meaning to see if it makes sense.

From Lubliner, S. (2001). *A practical guide to reciprocal teaching* (pp. 34, 39). Bothell, WA: Wright Group/McGraw-Hill; adapted by permission.

Getting Into Words: Vocabulary Instruction that Strengthens Comprehension by Shira Lubliner (with Linda Smetana)

TARJETA CON CLAVES
PARA CLARIFICAR CON ATRAPE UN COGNADO
(Spanish Translation of Clarifying Cue Card with Catch a Cognate)

Cuando encuentre una palabra que no entiende, use las estratégias siguientes:

USE SU MEMORIA

¿Ha visto esta palabra antes? ¿Recuerda qué significa?

ESTUDIE LA ESTRUCTURA

¿Sabe la raíz o base? ¿La palabra tiene un prefijo o sufijo que conoce? Use claves reconocidas en la palabra para adivinar el significado.

CONSIDERE EL CONTEXTO

Fije en la información en la oración y el párrafo. ¿Puede adivinar el significado?

SUSTITUYA UN SINÓNIMO

Si piensa que sabe el significado de la palabra, trate de poner una palabra con significado parecido en la oración. ¿Tiene sentido?

Si las estratégias no le resultan, trate lo siguiente:

PREGÚNTELE A UN EXPERTO

¿Alguien en su grupo sabrá lo que la palabra significa? Trabajando junto ¿pueden adivinar el significado?

PÓNGALE UN POST-IT

Si no puede adivinar el significado de la palabra, ponga un Post-It junto la palabra y pregúntele a la maestra o busque la palabra en el diccionario.

ATRAPE UN COGNADO

¿La palabra parece o suena como una palabra que conoce en español? Use el significado de la palabra en español para ver si tiene sentido.

From Lubliner, S. (2001). *A practical guide to reciprocal teaching* (pp. 34, 39). Bothell, WA: Wright Group/McGraw-Hill; translated and adapted by permission.

TARJETA CON CLAVES: ESTUDIE LA ESTRUCTURA
(Spanish Translation of Study the Structure Cue Card)

Cuando encuentre una palabra que no entiende, use la estratégia siguiente:

ESTUDIE LA ESTRUCTURA

Trate de ayudarse usando la estructura de la palabra (como está construida). ¿Sabe la raíz de la palabra? ¿Tiene un prefijo o sufijo que usted conoce? Trate de usar claves en la palabra para adivinar la palabra.

La base de la palabra

La base se usa para construir varias otras palabras. Cuando encuentre una palabra que no conoce, busque la base de la palabra para ver si le ayuda a adivinar el significado.

La raíz

Muchas palabras en inglés tienen raíces griegas o latinas. La raíz puede ayudarle a adivinar el significado de la palabra. Fije en la lista de raíces griegas y latinas para ver.

El prefijo

El prefijo se encuentra al principio de la palabra y ayuda a determinar su significado. ¿La palabra desconocida tiene un prefijo que usted conoce?

El sufijo

Un sufijo se encuentra al final de la palabra y ayuda a determinar su significado. ¿Tiene la palabra un sufijo que usted conoce?

UNA FOTO

Imagine que usted tiene una cámera. Tome una foto de la palabra y la oración que contiene la palabra para que usted recuerde la palabra cuando la vea otra vez. Cada vez que vea la palabra será más fácil recordarla.

TARJETA CON CLAVES: CONSIDERE EL CONTEXTO
(Spanish Translation of Consider the Context Cue Card)

Cuando encuentre una palabra que no entiende, use la estratégia siguiente:

CONSIDERE EL CONTEXTO

Lea la oración. ¿Tiene claves sobre el significado de la palabra? Lea el párrafo entero. ¿Ahora puede determinar lo que significa la palabra? ¡No se dé por vencido! Puede ser que necesite leer más para obtener más información sobre la palabra. Use las siguientes claves en el contexto como guías.

Busque claves entre comas.

A veces claves se esconden entre comas. Aquí hay un ejemplo: *El extraterrestre, un habitante de otro planeta, saltó de la nave espacial.* Note que la definición de la palabra *extraterrestre* está entre las comas.

Busque claves con explicaciones.

Aquí hay un ejemplo: *El curandero estaba preocupado. La gente de la tribu tenía fé en su habilidad para curarlos. Pero muchas personas se enfermaron y sus curamientos no funcionaban.* Note que la palabra *curandero* está explicada en las oraciones que siguen después de la palabra.

Busque claves con sentimientos.

Aquí hay un ejemplo: *Anoche sentí temor. Estaba en casa solo cuando empezó la tormenta. Se fue la luz. Relámpagos chocaban y truenos sacudían la casa.* Note que la palabra *temor* está explicada por oraciones que describen un susto.

Busque claves con palabras opuestas *como pero, sino, sin embargo y aunque.*

Claves en el contexto a veces se esconden. Aquí hay un ejemplo: *Estaba muy cansada, pero no pude dormir por el llanto del bebé.* Note que la palabra opuesta *pero* señala que una clave está escondida en la frase que sigue después de la palabra opuesta.

Getting Into Words: Vocabulary Instruction that Strengthens Comprehension
by Shira Lubliner (with Linda Smetana)

CATCH A COGNATE CUE CARD

Cognates are words that look or sound alike in two languages and mean nearly the same thing. There are many Spanish–English cognates. When you learn how to catch cognates, you will understand a lot of new words in English.

When you find an English word you don't understand, follow these steps:

LOOK AND LISTEN

Look at the English word. Does it *look* like a word you know in Spanish? Read it aloud. Does it *sound* like a Spanish word?

CONSIDER IT

Do you know what the word means in Spanish?

TRY IT

Read the whole sentence, using the Spanish word instead of the word in English.

THINK ABOUT IT

Think about it! Does the word make sense in the sentence? If it makes sense it's a cognate!

Celebrate! You've caught a cognate and learned a new word!

Getting Into Words: Vocabulary Instruction that Strengthens Comprehension
by Shira Lubliner (with Linda Smetana)

TARJETA CON CLAVES: ATRAPE UN COGNADO
(Spanish Translation of Catch a Cognate Cue Card)

Cognados son palabras que parecen y suenan similar en dos idiomas y tienen un significado muy similar. Hay muchos cognados español–inglés. Cuando aprenda a atrapar cognados, va a entender muchas más palabras en inglés.

Cuando vea una palabra en inglés que no entiende, siga los siguientes pasos:

MIRE Y ESCUCHE

Mire la palabra en inglés. ¿Se ve como una palabra que conoce en español? Lea la palabra en voz alta. ¿Suena como una palabra que conoce en español?

CONSIDERE

¿Sabe lo que la palabra significa en español?

INTENTE

Lea la oración completa usando la palabra en español en lugar de la palabra en inglés.

PIENSE

¡Piense! ¿Tiene sentido la palabra en la oración? Si tiene sentido, ¡es un cognado!

¡Celebre! ¡Atrapó un cognado y aprendió una palabra nueva!

Getting Into Words: Vocabulary Instruction that Strengthens Comprehension
by Shira Lubliner (with Linda Smetana)
161

Name: _____ Date: _____

CATCH A COGNATE WORKSHEET

Many of the words we use in school are similar in Spanish and English. For example, the word **similar** *is exactly the same in both languages. Use the Catch a Cognate Cue Card to help you figure out if an unknown word is a cognate. Here is an example:* **Her heart beat rapidly after running to class.**

1. **Look and listen.** Look at the word *rapidly.* Does it look like a word you know in Spanish? Does it *sound* like a Spanish word? Could it be a cognate?

   Rapidly looks and sounds a lot like the word rápido *in Spanish.*

2. **Consider it.** Do you know what the word means in Spanish?

   The word rápido *in Spanish means fast.*

3. **Try it.** Read the whole sentence using the Spanish word instead of the word in English.

   Her heart beat was rápido *after running to class.*

4. **Think about it.** Does the word make sense in a sentence?

   Yes, rápido *makes sense in the sentence. I think it's a cognate!*

Work with a partner and find each of the English cognates for the Spanish words in parentheses. Follow the steps on the Catch a Cognate Cue Card.

1. The cave paintings were made by prehistoric people. (*prehistórico*)

2. Discuss the characteristics of the people in the New England colonies.

   (*característicos*)

3. What is the correct abbreviation for the state of California? (*abreviatura*)

4. Find the congruent shapes. (*congruente*)

5. Write the definition of each word. (*definición*)

With your partner, identify cognates for the underlined words using the Catch a Cognate Cue Card.

1. Explain how the <u>system</u> works.

2. <u>Combine</u> these numbers.

3. <u>Describe</u> the character in the story.

4. What does this <u>symbol</u> mean?

5. Give <u>biographical</u> information about yourself.

Write some sentences of your own, using words that are cognates. Give your sentences to a friend and ask him or her to catch your cognates.

_____

_____

_____

_____

Getting Into Words: Vocabulary Instruction that Strengthens Comprehension
by Shira Lubliner (with Linda Smetana)

Part VI

Managing a Comprehensive Vocabulary Development Program

Chapter 11

Teaching Vocabulary Across the Curriculum and Throughout the School

When I entered Ms. Ryan's fifth-grade class at Bayside Elementary School, Katie immediately caught my attention. She appeared angry, with her arms crossed over her chest, and was glaring at the teacher. When Ms. Ryan introduced the lesson and asked the children to follow along, Katie refused to open her book. Later, when the children were reading and answering questions on a worksheet, Katie was disruptive, talking loudly and attempting to distract other children. Ms. Ryan spoke to her patiently, explaining the need to work quietly, but was unable to persuade Katie to attempt the assignment.

Later that day, I met with Ms. Evans, the school's reading specialist, to discuss a research study I hoped to conduct at Bayside the following year. I was interested in hearing more about the students I had observed earlier that day. I described my visit to Ms. Ryan's class and asked, "What can you tell me about Katie?"

Ms. Evans sighed. "I've known Katie for a long time. She entered Bayside as a first grader, with no previous preschool or kindergarten experience. Her first-grade teacher spoke to me early in the year and told me that Katie could not identify any of the letters or numbers and was unable to write her own name. The teacher was also concerned about Katie's poor oral language development. Her vocabulary was limited and her syntax was very underdeveloped for a 6-year-old child. Katie used phrases such as "Her wants to go."

"What kind of help did Katie get?" I asked.

Ms. Evans told me about the special reading program she had designed to support the students considered at risk of academic failure. She explained how she had tried to help Katie. "We began by referring Katie to the resource teacher to be tested for learning disabilities. Katie's scores were in the low-normal range, but we didn't find any evidence of learning disabilities. So, we enrolled her in our remedial reading program and brought her into the reading room for intensive instruction, 5 days per week. We taught her to decode with an explicit phonics program, and she gradually caught up with the rest of the class. We continued to work with her for several years. By the end of second grade, Katie was reading decodable texts, and her reading scores were within the low-average range. I was sure that the early intervention program had succeeded."

"It sounds like a great program!" I commented. "When did Katie become so angry and resistant to instruction?"

Ms. Evans explained that she had had little contact with Katie in the third grade because Katie did not qualify for any special services in that grade. But when Katie entered fourth grade, her performance dropped precipitously. According to Ms. Evans, Katie simply "crashed" in fourth grade. She struggled to complete assignments and failed comprehension tests. Ms. Evans explained further, "The fourth-grade teacher was concerned and asked me to test Katie to see if I could determine what was wrong. I called Katie to the reading room and asked her to read a story from the fourth-grade basal reader. She read the story accurately but with little expression. When I asked her a question about the main idea of the story, Katie ran her finger across the page, struggling to make sense of the words. At last she located a familiar word and came up with an answer, but it had nothing to do with the question I had asked. I realized that she did not understand anything she read. I wanted to help Katie, but my time was reserved for struggling first and second graders. I guess her teacher did not know what to do with her, and Katie fell further and further behind the class. By the end of the school year, Katie was so resistant to reading that she would not even try to complete text-based assignments. She also started getting into a lot of trouble."

"Why do you think Katie 'crashed' in fourth grade?" I asked.

Ms. Evans thought for a while and then responded. "I think Katie had serious vocabulary deficits when she started first grade. But I was focused on teaching her to read, and I did not realize that limited vocabulary was such an important problem. I taught her how to decode, and she made a lot of progress in reading. It didn't occur to me that she could only read the controlled-vocabulary books used in the primary grades."

"So you're saying that Katie only learned to read very easy books? I asked.

Ms. Evans nodded. "In the upper elementary grades, children have to read textbooks and novels with a lot of very difficult words. It's obvious to me now that the intervention did not solve Katie's reading problem because we did not teach her the vocabulary she needed to comprehend upper-grade books. So, now Katie is failing every subject and has a discipline problem, too. We've scheduled a student study team meeting next week to try to come up with a plan to help her. Do you have any suggestions?"

Ms. Evans and I talked at length about Katie and came up with some ideas that we thought would help. Ms. Evans met with Katie's mother, the fifth-grade teacher, and the resource specialist. The student study team discussed Katie's low reading comprehension and vocabulary test scores and agreed that vocabulary limitations were an important factor in Katie's reading problems. An intervention was designed and implemented.

HELPING KATIE

Katie was immersed in reading. Her mother agreed to restrict Katie's television viewing and to encourage her to read the high-interest leveled texts provided by the school. Ms. Ryan, Katie's teacher, monitored Katie's independent reading, asking Katie to retell the stories and to keep track of her retelling scores on a progress chart. Katie was paired with a high-achieving student for reading activities conducted in class and went to the resource room for extra help with her social studies assignments.

Ms. Evans changed her schedule so that she could meet regularly with Katie and several other struggling upper-elementary students. She taught the children to use the clarifying strategies (see Chapter 2) and helped them learn to monitor their own word learning (see Chapters 4–6). The fifth-grade teacher explicitly taught high-utility words that the children needed to know and engaged the children in word games and activities. The resource teacher, Ms. Evans, and Ms. Ryan kept in frequent contact with Katie's mother and closely monitored Katie's progress. Katie's behavior and attitude toward learning began to improve, and Katie put more effort into her school work. Her mother and teachers hoped that the intervention would also result in substantial improvement in her academic performance.

I returned to Bayview the following year to begin preparations for a research study based on my vocabulary intervention. I knew that there were many struggling readers like Katie at Bayside. The school was located in a low-income urban community. Few of the families could afford to send their children to preschool, so kindergarten or first grade was often the children's first structured educational experience. Many of the disadvantaged children, like Katie, entered school with vocabulary limitations that interfered with reading. Despite a carefully designed early intervention program, many serious reading problems emerged in the upper elementary grades. The principal and Ms. Evans recognized the need for improved instruction and supported my suggestion that we conduct a vocabulary intervention at Bayside.

The fifth-grade teachers and I met a few weeks later to discuss the intervention. I discussed recent research findings with them, explaining that disadvantaged children often enter school with substantial vocabulary limitations that grow wider each year. I pointed out that children need powerful vocabulary instruction that is designed to foster deep word-level knowledge in order to positively affect their reading comprehension. We also discussed word-learning strategies and the importance of teaching children to monitor their own comprehension.

THE BAYSIDE STUDY

We began the study by administering a series of pretests designed to provide baseline information about the children's vocabulary and reading comprehension. We asked the teachers to provide normal instruction for a period of 12 weeks and then administered interim vocabulary and reading comprehension tests. We planned to compare the results of the first 12 weeks of normal instruction (the control period) with the results of 12 weeks of comprehensive vocabulary development instruction (the experimental period). We also compared the children's achievement with that of children in a much higher-performing school.

At the end of the first 12-week period, I met with the fifth-grade teachers and introduced the comprehensive vocabulary development program. I conducted several training sessions, instructing the teachers how to implement the program and providing them with instructional materials (the lesson plans, worksheets, and cue cards addressing the three dimensions of vocabulary knowledge contained in this book). Then I visited the fifth-grade classrooms and modeled clarifying strategy lessons with the students.

A Model Lesson

My first model lesson took place on a Wednesday morning in Ms. Ryan's class. I began with the Clarifying Cue Card (see p. 38), carefully modeling each strategy with a text selection and thinking aloud so that the children could follow my reasoning. I showed the children examples of Mine Your Memory, Study the Structure, and Consider the Context clues and demonstrated the use of Substitute a Synonym to ensure that the understanding of word meaning is correct. I placed a transparency containing a paragraph from the children's social studies book on the overhead and read the following sentence: *The new land was wild and <u>unexplored</u>.* I pointed to the underlined word, *unexplored,* and showed the children how they could clarify it using the strategies on their Clarifying Cue Card. We agreed that a combination of Mine Your Memory (remember the word *explore* from previous social studies lessons) and Study the Structure (identify the negative prefix *un-*) were the most helpful strategies and provided good information about word meaning. I uncovered the next paragraph from the social studies textbook on the transparency and read the following sentence: *The colonists were <u>mystified</u> by many Native American customs.* I pointed to the underlined word, *mystified.* "Now you try it! Use your clarifying strategies to make sense of the word!" I said, smiling at the children. Thirty-one pairs of eyes gazed back at me attentively, but no one tried to clarify the word.

"Hmm," I thought to myself, "This is not going well." Although the children were well behaved and engaged when I provided direct instruction, they did not respond when I asked them to implement the strategies themselves. "The instruction must have been inadequate," I decided. "I released responsibility too soon." So, I taught the process again, carefully modeling each step. I read another sentence from the paragraph on the transparency and asked the children to identify a challenging word. I underlined the word the children identified and asked them to select a strategy that would help us make sense of the word. With my help, the children successfully clarified the word and substituted a synonym. Now, I was sure they would be able to carry out the process themselves.

I asked the children to open their social studies book to the page we had been discussing. "I want you to read the next paragraph in the book, and do the same thing I just showed you. Find a difficult word and use your clarifying strategies to help you figure out what it means. Work together and talk about the words. Does everyone understand? Okay, get started!"

Only a few children began to read the text. The rest stared blankly at me, clearly baffled by my instructions. Finally, Diego, a boy seated at the first table group, raised his hand. "Why don't you just tell us the words we don't know? Then we can look them up like we always do."

My heart sank! I thought to myself, "This is going to be a challenge!" I realized that the children were accustomed to traditional vocabulary instruction based on explicit instruction and dictionary assignments. The children expected to be told words to look up and learn, rather than to learn to implement independent word learning strategies. It was clear that teaching these children the latter would entail major changes in the teachers' instructional practices.

Changing Instructional Practices

Later that afternoon I met with the three fifth-grade teachers, Ms. Ryan, Ms. Sullivan, and Ms. Judd, and the school reading specialist, Ms. Evans, to discuss the vocabulary development program that we were beginning to implement. Ms. Ryan, Ms. Sullivan, and Ms. Judd trudged into the meeting, tired after a long day of teaching. Despite their exhaustion, the teachers were resolute in their determination to learn new methods of vocabulary instruction that could help their students. We discussed the children's passive behavior and the difficulty I had engaging them in word-learning activities. The teachers explained that most of the children came from very poor homes and had little exposure to reading before entering school. Few students had attended preschool, and many spoke languages other than English at home. Ms. Evans, the reading specialist, explained that many years of poor academic performance had worn the children down. As she put it, "They've just stopped trying." According to Ms. Evans, many of the teachers in this Title I school responded to their demoralized students by taking responsibility for the children's learning upon themselves. The children knew that if they sat back and waited, the teachers would preteach the vocabulary, point out important ideas in the text, and tell them what they needed to remember. Their passivity was reinforced year after year by well-meaning teachers. By the time they entered fifth grade, the children had grown so dependent that it was nearly impossible to engage them in independent literacy activities.

The teachers and I acknowledged that it was going to be difficult to change ingrained learning habits, but we were determined to teach the children to take a more active role in the learning process. Vocabulary scores for most of the children were below the basic level, so we agreed that it was vital that the children read more, learn many words, and become independent word learners. Ms. Evans and I carefully reviewed the vocabulary materials (the Tools of Success) that I had developed and selected tools designed to teach each dimension of vocabulary knowledge. I organized the tools, providing the teachers with a sequence of instructional activities for the 12-week intervention. The teachers implemented the comprehensive vocabulary development program, providing vocabulary instruction during the 40-minute social studies period, two to three times per week.

Results of the Study

I returned to Bayside Elementary School a few weeks after the vocabulary program began and found many changes in the fifth-grade classes. The teachers were following the vocabulary development program and were gradually overcoming the children's resistance to active engagement with texts. The teachers insisted that the children monitor their own comprehension, implement strategies, and make sense of words for themselves. According to the teachers, allowing the children to implement vocabulary activities in collaborative groups was a key factor in the success of the program. The children enjoyed working together, increasing their persistence in carrying out assigned tasks. The teachers reported that the students were beginning to respond to the new methods.

Weeks went by and Ms. Ryan, Ms. Sullivan, and Ms. Judd persevered despite the children's resistance and the many demands imposed upon teachers in underperforming schools. They felt rewarded by signs that the vocabulary instruction was helping the children become better readers. At the end of 12 weeks of instruction, posttests were administered. The results demonstrated significant growth in the children's reading comprehension and vocabulary following the vocabulary intervention. Before the study, the children's scores had been compared with those of children in a higher-performing school. There were large, significant differences in scores that grew larger during the control period. Results of the final comparison of reading comprehension and vocabulary scores revealed small, insignificant differences between the Bayside children and the comparison group, suggesting a narrowing of the achievement gap. (For study data and statistical analysis, see Lubliner & Smetana, 2004.)

The results of the study were very encouraging. The teachers and I were particularly pleased that the children made significant gains in reading comprehension, an outcome that has rarely been documented in vocabulary studies (Beck et al., 2002; Nagy, 1985, 1988). We concluded that effective vocabulary instruction made a big difference at Bayside. The teachers were proud of their accomplishments and felt that the children were on the right track. The Bayside fifth graders were on their way to becoming independent word learners.

A Schoolwide Effort to Improve
Vocabulary and Reading Comprehension

Ms. Evans and fifth-grade teachers met with me again to review the results of the study and to discuss plans for the future. Although very pleased with their students' progress, the teachers were discouraged by the prospect of having to save so many struggling readers each year.

Ms. Ryan commented, "I think that the only way we can prevent kids from 'crashing' in the upper elementary grades is to make sure they learn a lot more vocabulary in the lower grades. I know that it's really important to teach reading and that the lower-grade teachers are under a lot of pressure. But I feel like all they care about is decoding skills. They don't seem to realize how important it is to teach vocabulary. So, the kids learn to read, but they don't learn the words they need to understand what they are reading. By the time the kids get to fourth or fifth grade it's too late."

"I don't think it's too late." I told Ms. Ryan. "You did a great job this year, and the children really benefited from the vocabulary program. But you're right that it would be a lot easier and more effective if the primary teachers did their share of vocabulary instruction. It's going to take a schoolwide effort to solve Bayside's achievement problems. You'll need carefully planned vocabulary instruction year after year to bring these kids to a point that they can read and comprehend upper-grade textbooks."

The fifth-grade teachers shared the results of the vocabulary study with their colleagues. They explained that vocabulary deficits were not being addressed in the primary grades, contributing to upper-grade reading failure. The faculty agreed that a schoolwide effort to strengthen children's vocabulary development was needed. Figure 11.1 shows an instructional scope and sequence chart that can be used as a framework for a schoolwide vocabulary development program.

A schoolwide vocabulary development program requires teachers and administrators to work together to ensure that children acquire the vocabulary that they need. Each year, teachers build on the foundation of prior year's instruction. They

Instructional Scope and Sequence for Implementing the Tools of Success

Grade	Procedural knowledge (clarifying strategies)	Conditional knowledge (self-monitoring and self-regulation)	Declarative knowledge (in-depth word knowledge)
Kindergarten	Beginning use of Mine Your Memory	Answering simple prompts such as "Do you know that word? and "How do you know?"	Repeated read-aloud of high-interest stories Use of new words in classroom discourse
First grade	Beginning use of Mine Your Memory Beginning use of Study the Structure and Consider the Context	Self-monitoring with Stop Sign when text is read aloud in large groups	Repeated read-aloud of high-interest stories Use of new words in classroom discourse Use of Picture Prediction before reading
Second grade	Use of clarifying strategies based on Clarifying Cue Card for Kids	Self-monitoring with Stop Sign when text is read aloud in large groups	Repeated read-aloud of high-interest stories Use of new words in classroom discourse Use of Picture Prediction before reading
Third grade	Use of clarifying strategies based on the Clarifying Cue Card for Kids	Self-monitoring with Stop Sign when text is read aloud in large groups Use of Stoplight Vocabulary	Repeated read-aloud of high-interest stories Use of new words in classroom discourse Use of Picture Prediction before reading Beginning use of graphic organizers such as semantic maps for important vocabulary words
Fourth grade	Use of clarifying strategies based on the Clarifying Cue Card Emphasis on Study the Structure	Self-monitoring with Stop Sign during independent reading Use of Stoplight Vocabulary	Read-aloud of books with rich vocabulary Use of new words in classroom discourse Beginning use of Title Prediction and Sorting Use of graphic organizers for important vocabulary words: Semantic Maps, Feature Analysis Charts, Word Scales Use of Mental Imagery
Fifth to eighth grades	Use of clarifying strategies based on the Clarifying Cue Card Emphasis on Consider the Context, especially Be a Super Sleuth and activities based on signal words	Self-monitoring with Stoplight Vocabulary Use of the Zone of Comprehension Self-regulation (selecting and implementing clarifying strategies during independent reading) Use of the Clarifying Strategy Decision Tree	Read-aloud of books with rich vocabulary Use of new words in classroom discourse Use of Title Prediction and Sorting Use of graphic organizers for important vocabulary words: Semantic Maps, Feature Analysis Charts, Word Scales Use of Mental Imagery Use of Word Study Journal Use of Getting Into Words with Poetry

Figure 11.1. Suggested instructional scope and sequence for implementing the Tools of Success from kindergarten through eighth grade. (Actual scope and sequence varies based on a teacher's assessment of the students' specific needs.)

reinforce the Tools of Success and teach children more words and increasingly sophisticated methods of word learning. Implementing a schoolwide vocabulary development program pays off in a variety of ways. Children emerge from passive dependence on teachers and take responsibility for their own word learning. Their vocabulary acquisition accelerates as they use clarifying strategies in independent reading. Over time, a schoolwide vocabulary development program can narrow the achievement gap, contributing to the success of all children.

FINAL THOUGHTS

Schools demand a great deal from teachers, asking them to nurture, test, teach, and prepare children for success in a rapidly changing world. The pressure on teachers grows ever greater as our knowledge base expands. Technology has changed the way we process information and evolves with lightening speed. The medium of communication, however, remains the same as it has been throughout the millennia: We communicate with words. We use words to read, write, listen, and speak with one another. Words are the vehicle we use to entertain, to inform, and to express our needs.

Children need to learn a vast number of words and rely on teachers to provide them with the means to acquire these essential tools of communication. Teaching children to get into words is much more than teaching test-taking skills. When children get into words, they acquire the building blocks of knowledge, allowing them to share meaningful ideas. Providing children with rich vocabulary and independent word-learning skills prepares them for success in higher education and gives them the ability to receive and share information in an everchanging world.

References

Armento, B., Nash, G.B., Salter, C.L., & Wixson, K.K. (1991). *America will be.* Boston: Houghton Mifflin.

Ayers, D.M. (1986). *English words from Latin and Greek elements* (2nd ed., rev. by T.D. Worthen, with R.L. Cherry). Tucson: University of Arizona Press.

Baker, S. (1995). *Vocabulary instruction: Synthesis of the research* (Tech. Rep. No. 13). Eugene, OR: National Center to Improve the Tools of Education.

Baumann, J.F., Kame'enui, E.J., & Ash, G. (2003). Research on vocabulary instruction: Voltaire redux. In J. Flood, D. Lapp, J. Jensen, & J.R. Squire (Eds.), *Handbook of research on teaching the English language arts* (2nd ed., pp. 752–787). New York: Macmillan.

Beck, I., McKeown, M., & Kucan, L. (2002). *Bringing words to life.* New York: The Guilford Press.

Biemiller, A. (1999). *Language and reading success.* Cambridge, MA: Brookline Books.

Biemiller, A. (2004). Teaching vocabulary in the primary grades: Vocabulary instruction needed. In J. Baumann & E. Kame'enui (Eds.), *Vocabulary instruction: Research to practice.* New York: The Guilford Press.

Blake, M. (1996). *Monsters of the deep.* Bothell, WA: Wright Group/McGraw-Hill.

Brocker, S. (2000). *Against all odds.* Bothell, WA: Lands End Publishing, a division of The Wright Group.

Carey, S. (1978). The child as a word learner. In M. Halle, J. Bresnan, & G. Miller (Eds.), *Linguistic theory and psychological reality* (pp. 264–293). Cambridge, MA: The MIT Press.

Cannon, J. (1993). *Stellaluna.* Orlando, FL: Harcourt.

Chall, J.S., Jacobs, V.A., & Baldwin, L.E. (1990). *The reading crisis: Why poor children fall behind.* Cambridge, MA: Harvard University Press.

Dale, E. (1965). Vocabulary measurement: Techniques and major findings. *Elementary English, 42,* 82–88.

Dale, E., & O'Rourke, J. (1981). *The living word vocabulary.* Chicago: World Book/Childcraft International.

de Paola, T. (1975). *Strega Nona.* Upper Saddle River, NJ: Prentice Hall.

Freebody, P., & Anderson, R. (1983). Effects of differing proportions and locations of difficult vocabulary on text comprehension. *Journal of Reading Behavior, 15,* 19–39.

Fukkink, R., & de Glopper, K. (1998). Effects of instruction in deriving word meanings from context: A meta-analysis. *Review of Educational Research, 68,* 450–469.

Galdone, P. (1985). *The little red hen.* Boston: Houghton Mifflin.

Gambrell, L., Morrow, L., Neuman, S., & Pressley, M. (Eds.). (1999). *Best practices in literacy instruction.* New York: The Guilford Press.

Ganske, K. (2000). *Word journeys.* New York: The Guilford Press.

Graves, M. (1984). Selecting vocabulary to teach in the intermediate and secondary grades. In J. Flood (Ed.), *Promoting reading comprehension* (pp. 245–260). Newark, DE: International Reading Association.

Graves, M. (1987). The roles of instruction in fostering vocabulary development. In M. McKeown & M. Curtis (Eds.), *The nature of vocabulary acquisition* (pp. 165–184). Mahwah, NJ: Lawrence Erlbaum Associates.

Graves, M.F. (2000). A vocabulary program to complement and bolster a middle grade comprehension program. In B.M. Taylor, M.F. Graves, & P. van den Broek (Eds.), *Reading for meaning: Fostering comprehension in the middle grades.* Newark, DE: International Reading Association.

Guthrie, J.T., & Humenick, N.M. (2003). Motivating students to read: Evidence for classroom practices that increase reading motivation and achievement. In P. McCardle & V. Chhabra (Eds.), *The voice of evidence in reading research* (pp. 329–354). Baltimore: Paul H. Brookes Publishing Co.

Hammer, P. (1979). *What is the use of cognates?* Washington, DC: U.S. Department of Health, Education and Welfare. (ERIC Document Reproduction Service No. ED180202)

Hart, B., & Risley, T.R. (1995). *Meaningful differences in the everyday experiences of young American children.* Baltimore: Paul H. Brookes Publishing Co.

Hart, B., & Risley, T.R. (1999). *The social world of children learning to talk.* Baltimore: Paul H. Brookes Publishing Co.

Henry, M.K. (2003). *Unlocking literacy: Effective spelling and decoding instruction.* Baltimore: Paul H. Brookes Publishing Co.

Hirsch, E.D., Jr. (2003, Spring). Reading comprehension requires knowledge of words and the world: Scientific insights into the fourth-grade slump and the nation's stagnant comprehension scores. *American Educator,* 10–45.

Kamil, M.L. (2004). Vocabulary and comprehension instruction: Summary and implications of the National Reading Panel findings. In P. McCardle & V. Chhabra (Eds.), *The voice of evidence in reading research* (pp. 213–234). Baltimore: Paul H. Brookes Publishing Co.

Kindler, A.L. (2002). *Survey of the states' limited English proficient students and available educational programs and services: 2000–2001 summary report.* Washington, DC: National Clearinghouse for English Language Acquisition and Language Instruction Educational Programs.

Levey, J. (Ed.). (1989). *Macmillan dictionary for children.* New York: Macmillan.

Lindbergh, R. (1990). *The day the goose got loose* (S. Kellogg, Illus.). New York: The Penguin Group.

Lord, B.B. (1984). *In the year of the boar and Jackie Robinson* (M. Simont, Illus.). New York: HarperCollins.

Lubliner, S. (2001). *A practical guide to reciprocal teaching.* Bothell, WA: Wright Group/McGraw-Hill.

Lubliner, S., & Smetana, L. (2004, June 23). *The effects of comprehensive vocabulary instruction on the metacognitive word-learning skills and reading comprehension of disadvantaged students.* Manuscript submitted for publication.

McKeown, M. (1993). Creating effective definitions for young word learners. *Reading Research Quarterly, 28*(1), 16–31.

Nagy, W. (1985). *Vocabulary instruction: Implications of the new research.* Paper presented at the convention of the National Council of Teachers of English, Philadelphia.

Nagy, W. (1988). *Vocabulary instruction and reading comprehension.* (Tech. Rep. No. 431). Urbana: Illinois University, Center for the Study of Reading.

Nagy, W., Anderson, R., & Herman, P. (1986). *The influence of word and text properties on learning from context.* Urbana: Illinois University, Center for the Study of Reading (ERIC Document Reproduction Service No. ED266443).

Nagy, W., & Herman, P. (1984). *Limitations of vocabulary instruction* (Tech. Rep. No. 326). Urbana: Illinois University, Center for the Study of Reading.

Nagy, W. & Herman, P. (1987). Breadth and depth of vocabulary knowledge: Implications for acquisition and instruction. In M. McKeown & M. Curtis (Eds.) *The nature of vocabulary acquisition* (pp. 19–36). Mahwah, NJ: Lawrence Erlbaum Associates.

Nagy, W., & Scott, J. (2000). Vocabulary processes. In M.L. Kamil, P.B. Mosenthal, P.D. Pearson, & R. Barr (Eds.), *Handbook of reading research* (Vol. III, pp. 269–284). Mahwah, NJ: Lawrence Erlbaum Associates.

Nash, R. (1997). *NTC's dictionary of Spanish cognates.* Chicago: NTC Publishing Group.

National Institute of Child Health and Human Development. (2000). *Teaching children to read: An evidence-based assessment of the scientific research literature on reading and its implications for reading instruction* (NIH Publication No. 00-4769). Washington, DC: U.S. Government Printing Office.

Noyes, A. (1907). *Forty singing seamen and other poems.* Edinburgh and London: William Blackwood & Sons.

O'Dell, S. (1960). *Island of the blue dolphins.* Boston: Houghton Mifflin.

Palincsar, A. (1983). *Reciprocal teaching of comprehension-monitoring activities* (Rep. No. US NIE-C-400-76-0116). Washington DC: U.S. Department of Education.

Palincsar, A. (1985). *The unpacking of a multi-component, metacognitive training package.* Paper presented at the annual meeting of the American Educational Research Association, Chicago.

Pearson, D., & Dole, J. (1987). Explicit comprehension instruction: A review of research and a new conceptualization of instruction. *Journal of Learning Disabilities, 25,* 211–225, 229.

Pressley, M., Woloshyn, V., Burkell, J., Cariglia-Bull, T., Lysynchuk, L., McGoldrick, J., et al. (1995). *Cognitive strategy instruction that really improves children's academic performance.* Cambridge, MA: Brookline Books.

Rosenshine, B. (1997). *The case for explicit teacher-led cognitive strategy instruction.* Paper presented at the annual meeting of the American Educational Research Association, Chicago.

Ruddell, M.R. (1994). Vocabulary knowledge and comprehension: A comprehension-process view of complex literacy relationships. In R. Ruddell, M.R. Ruddell, & H. Singer (Eds.), *Theoretical models and processes of reading* (4th ed., pp. 414–437). Newark, DE: International Reading Association.

Schlissel, L. (1995). *Black frontiers: A history of African American heroes in the Old West.* New York: Aladdin Paperbacks.

Scott, J., & Nagy, W. (2004). Developing word consciousness. In J. Baumann & E. Kame'enui (Eds.), *Vocabulary instruction: Research to practice.* New York: The Guilford Press.

Stahl, S. (1989). Task variations and prior knowledge in learning word meanings from context. In S. McCormick & J. Zutell (Eds.), *Thirty-eighth yearbook of the National Reading Conference* (pp. 197–203). Chicago: National Reading Conference.

Stahl, S.A., & Fairbanks, M.M. (1986). The effects of vocabulary instruction: A model-based meta-analysis. *Review of Educational Research, 56,* 72–110.

Stanovich, K.E. (1986). Matthew effects in reading: Some consequences of individual differences in the acquisition of literacy. *Reading Research Quarterly, 21,* 360–406.

Stein, J. (Ed.). (1975). *The Random House college dictionary* (Rev. ed.). Toronto: Random House.

Swanborn, M.S.L., & de Glopper, K. (1999). Incidental word learning while reading: A meta-analysis. *Review of Educational Research, 69,* 261–285.

Time Inc. (2002). Time for Kids world report [Special issue]. *Go Places with TFK, 8*(78).

Viorst, J. (1972). *Alexander and the terrible, horrible, no good, very bad day* (R. Cruz, Illus.). New York: Atheneum.

Vygotsky, L.S. (1978). *Mind in society: The development of higher psychological processes* (M. Cole, V. John-Steiner, S. Scribner, & E. Souberman, Eds. and Trans.). Cambridge, MA: Harvard University Press.

Wallace, K. (1998). *Tale of a tadpole.* New York: DK Publishing.

White, T., Power, M., & White, S. (1989). Morphological analysis: Implications for teaching and understanding vocabulary growth. *Reading Research Quarterly, 24,* 283–304.

White, T., Sowell, J., & Yanagihara, A. (1989). Growth of reading vocabulary in diverse elementary schools. *Reading Teacher, 42,* 343–354.

Zeno, S.M., Ivens, S.H., Millard, R.T., & Duvvuri, R. (1995). *The educator's word frequency guide.* New York: Touchstone Applied Science Associates & National Institute of Child Health and Human Development.

Glossary

affix A word part that is added to the beginning (prefix) or end (suffix) of a base word or root to create a new word. *See also* prefix, suffix.

artificially designed text A contrived text designed to support the acquisition of a specific strategy or to provide practice of a specific strategy.

authentic text A text created by an author for the purpose of informing, entertaining, persuading, and so forth. Authentic texts may include trade books, newspapers, primary source documents, essays, and informational texts.

basal reader The student book found in a basal reading program that includes a teacher's manual, workbooks, and assessments. These programs are developed around a scope and sequence designed to meet state or national standards.

base word A word to which prefixes and/or suffixes may be added to create a new word; unlike roots, base words can stand alone as words without affixes.

background knowledge Knowledge and experiences a student has connected to a subject.

bound morpheme *See* morpheme.

challenging text Text that is difficult for the reader to understand because it contains many new vocabulary words, requires specific background knowledge, presents unfamiliar concepts or content, and/or has complex sentence and paragraph structures.

clarify To make clearer by explaining in greater detail; clarifying words is the process of determining word meaning though memory, structure, or context.

cloze passage A short text with missing words (indicated by blanks). Students fill in the blanks with words that determine the meaning of the text. The purpose of using cloze passages is to sensitize students to nuances of word meaning so that they develop control over expressive vocabulary.

conceptual load The number and complexity of the concepts presented in a text. Texts that present several new concepts with new accompanying vocabulary have a higher conceptual load than texts that only present one new concept at a time. Texts that contain many unfamiliar and difficult to decode words also have a high conceptual load.

cognate A word that has the same linguistic root or origin as a target word and that may share some similarities in spelling, pronunciation, and meaning with the target word.

comprehension The process of constructing meaning from text; includes focusing on relevant information and integrating it with what one already knows. Comprehension is an active process in which readers set purposes for reading, actively process the text, and apply fix-up strategies when understanding breaks down.

conditional knowledge Knowledge of when to use strategies to regulate word learning.

considerate text Text that supplies enough information to the reader to facilitate comprehension and learning from reading. (Text that is too considerate presents so much textual guidance that the reader does not need to apply strategies to determine the meaning of unknown words. Overly considerate texts may define words in the page margins or through the use of parentheses and appositives.)

context Words, phrases or passages that come before and after a particular word or passage that help to explain a target word or passage.

contextual support Text written in such a manner that a reader can use the context to determine the meaning of unknown words.

controlled vocabulary text Text (often a series of texts) with a limited set of words that are repeated throughout.

cue card A card or a poster with information to prompt student use of strategies. A cue card is more extensive than a flash card.

declarative knowledge   Knowledge of *which* words one need to know.

decoding   The process of sounding out a word by translating the graphemes, or letters, into phonemes, or speech sounds. To decode the word *man* one would say /m/ /ă/ /n/. Decoding can also take place using larger linguistic units such as syllables.

derivational suffix   A suffix that changes a word from one part of speech to another. For example, adding *-ly* to the adjective *quick* creates the adverb *quickly*.

explicit instruction   Instruction that is expressed in a clear and obvious manner, leaving no doubt as to the intended meaning or process to be followed.

expressive vocabulary   An individual's speaking vocabulary; words used by an individual to express ideas, thoughts, and feelings.

false cognate   Words in two languages, such as Spanish and English, that have similar spelling and pronunciation yet have different meanings. For example *asistir* and *assist* are false cognates. *Asistir* means *to attend*; *assist* means *to help*. The word in Spanish for *to assist* is *ayudar*.

fluency   The ability to read accurately with appropriate speed and phrasing.

free morpheme   *See* morpheme.

frustration level   The level at which an individual cannot effectively read or comprehend text. The text may be too difficult due to the number of words that the reader does not recognize, the number of words whose meaning is not known to the reader, or the number of words whose concepts and meanings are not grasped by the reader.

graphic organizer   A visual structure for representing the ideas in a text. Frequently used graphic organizers include Venn diagrams, webs, story maps, arrays, and grids.

graphophonic   Pertaining to the knowledge and recognition of letters and their sound–spelling relationships. Learners who have graphophonic knowledge can blend sounds represented by letters into words, can segment separate words into their appropriate sounds, and can spell the target words.

guided practice   Part of a lesson in which the teacher provides opportunities for students to apply or practice the material under the teacher's supervision.

high frequency   When used with reference to words or roots, denotes those that are most common in connected text. High-frequency words include *if, an, the, for, when, after, is,* and *me.* High-frequency roots include *tri, graph,* and *tele.*

high utility   When used with reference to words or roots, denotes those that are frequent and useful to know.

incidental word learning   Word learning that takes place during reading without conscious effort, intention, or instruction.

independent word learning   Word learning that occurs through the use of strategies that a student can carry out on his or her own, without outside assistance. Independent word learning occurs without prompting, guidance, or assistance from the teacher.

infer   To make a conclusion about meaning on the basis of information given and reasoning.

inflectional suffix   A suffix that indicates verb tense, adjective or adverb comparison, or noun plurality or possession (e.g., *-ed, -ing, -es, -'s*).

intentional word learning   Purposeful word learning through the conscious application of effective strategies, including determining word knowledge and using reparative strategies until the word meaning is determined.

level of word learning   One's knowledge of understanding of words; this level progresses along a word-learning continuum from no knowledge, to partial concept and receptive word knowledge, to full concept and expressive word knowledge. *Also called* stage of word learning.

leveled text   Text, often books, stories, or articles, designed to be read by individuals with specific reading skills and strategies. Leveled text may include specifically designed text or text that has been determined to be able to be read by individuals with specific reading skills.

literacy   Ability to read and write.

manipulate   To move around, change, or exchange.

metacognition   Knowledge and self-regulation of one's own thinking and learning processes that enables a person to regulate deliberate efforts for effective reading and studying.

monitor   Check behaviors and/or understandings during the learning process.

morpheme The smallest unit of meaning in language; free morphemes (e.g., *cat, elephant*) are words and can stand alone; bound morphemes (e.g., *inter-, bio, -ing*), are affixes or roots that must be attached to other word parts to form words.

morphological support Used to describe a text containing many words whose meanings can be constructed through the identification of base words, roots, and affixes.

morphology Study of the structure of words, including word parts such as compounds, base words, roots, and affixes.

phoneme A single speech sound (e.g., /m/). Some phonemes are represented in writing by more than one letter (e.g., the single sound /ch/ is represented by the letters *ch*). Some phonemes may be represented in writing several different ways (e.g., /k/ can be spelled as *k, c, ck,* or *-que*).

prefix An affix that is added before a base word or root to create a new word. In English, prefixes are often of Greek (e.g., *chem-, poly-*) or Latin (e.g., *pro-, ex-*) origin. *See also* affix.

procedural knowledge Knowledge of *how* to use vocabulary acquisition strategies intentionally during reading.

proficient reader A reader who is able to read and comprehend grade-appropriate text. Proficient readers apply strategies for effective reading and are able to monitor their reading and make changes according to the nature of the text and their purposes for reading.

reading failure Inability to read at a level necessary in order to accomplish one's tasks and goals. The term encompasses an inability to read anything at all as well as competent decoding accompanied by lack of ability to comprehend what is meant. *Reading failure* can also mean inability to read age- or grade-level texts despite ability to comprehend much easier texts.

receptive vocabulary An individual's listening vocabulary; words that an individual understands and comprehends.

root A unit of meaning, usually of Greek or Latin origin, to which prefixes and/or suffixes are added to create a new word; roots are not usually complete words. *See also* base word; bound morpheme.

scaffolding Necessary support for learners provided through materials, instructional modeling, and practice.

self-monitoring Ability to check one's learning or reading, including monitoring of word knowledge and comprehension during the reading process. Self-monitoring includes being aware of one's own comprehension and aware of when it breaks down so that one can take reparative action. *See also* self-regulation.

self-regulation Ability to monitor one's learning and to implement the appropriate strategies or sequence of strategies to achieve cognitive goals or to respond to a breakdown in comprehension. Self-monitoring and self-regulation are sequential metacognitive tasks. First the child self-monitors and determines that there is an unknown word in the text. Then the child self-regulates, selecting the best strategy or strategies to make sense of the word and to restore comprehension of the text. *See also* self-monitoring.

semantic Relating to the meaning of or differences between meanings of words or phrases.

stage of word learning *See* level of word learning.

strategies When used with reference to reading, plans, processes, and behaviors that are used to achieve effective reading.

structural analysis A method for determining the meaning and pronunciation of word through an examination of the meaning units of the word. Often this process includes looking for affixes and base words or roots within the target word. For example, the word *quickly* can be broken into the base word *quick* and the suffix *-ly.*

struggling reader A reader who is not able to read and comprehend grade-appropriate text; usually a struggling reader lacks the strategies for effective reading and is reading at least one grade level behind his or her peers.

suffix An affix that is added after a base word or root to create a new word. In English, suffixes are often of Anglo-Saxon (e.g., *-dom, -ish, -ness*), Greek (e.g., *-logy*), or Latin (e.g., *-or, -ous, -tion*) origin. Sometimes words can have more than one suffix (e.g., *carelessness, fundamentally*). *See also* affix.

synonym A word whose meaning is the same or about the same as the target word in the particular context.

syntax The system governing the underlying structure of phrases and sentences, including the ordering of and relationship between words and punctuation in phrases and sentences.

target word A known or unknown word to be studied.

vocabulary Words, as single units or in phrases or sentences, that carry meaning. Writers chose a particular vocabulary to convey specific meanings. *See also* expressive vocabulary; receptive vocabulary.

word family Words that share the same base or root. For example *biology, biodiversity, biologist, biological,* and *biodegradable* share the root *bio,* which means *life.* The words *rerun, runner,* and *running* share the base word *run.*

word knowledge One's conceptual understanding of a word.

word parts Structural parts of a word, such as base words or roots, affixes, syllables, or chunks of words.

word structure How word parts are placed together to form a word.

word-learning continuum A continuum comprising several stages of word knowledge, from not knowing a word, to partial understanding, to complete conceptual understanding.

BIBLIOGRAPHY

Ganske, K. (2000). *Word journeys.* New York: The Guilford Press.

Henry, M.K. (2003). Unlocking literacy: *Efffective decoding and spelling instruction.* Baltimore: Paul H. Brookes Publishing Co.

Moats, L.C. (2000). *Speech to print: Language essentials for teachers.* Baltimore: Paul H. Brookes Publishing Co.

Radniski, T., & Padak, N. (2004). *Effective reading strategies* (3rd ed.). Upper Saddle River, NJ: Pearson.

Reutzel, R., & Cooter, R. (2003). *Strategies for reading assessment and instruction* (2nd ed.). Upper Saddle River, NJ: Merrill.

Appendix B

Answer Key

ALL IN THE FAMILY

*Word families are groups of words that are related to the same base word. If you know the base word, it is easy to find all of the relatives. Just look inside the word! In the example below, we read the story in the box and underline the words that belong to the **send** family. We write each word in the **send** family in the circle.*

SEND

sent
sends
sending
sender

I need to <u>send</u> a birthday card to my grandma. She always <u>sends</u> me a card and a present for my birthday. Last year I <u>sent</u> the card to the wrong address. It came back to me with the label returned to <u>sender</u>. This year I'm <u>sending</u> Grandma two cards, just in case I make a mistake!

*Read the story in the box below. Underline the words that are part of the **build**, **work**, and **employ** word families, and write them in the family circles.*

Ever since he was a little boy, Jason was interested in his dad's <u>work</u>. Jason's dad owned a construction company that <u>built</u> houses and apartments. He <u>employed</u> six <u>workers</u> who helped him. Jason always wanted to be a <u>builder</u> like his dad. He begged his dad to take him to <u>work</u>. But his dad said that a construction site was too dangerous for small children.

When Jason turned 10, his dad finally agreed to take him to <u>work</u>. On the first day of winter break, Jason and his dad went to see the new apartment house the company was <u>building</u>. They put on hard hats to protect their heads. Dad helped Jason climb into the lift that took them to the third floor. Dad had to discuss some problems with the manager. Meanwhile, Jason watched the <u>builders</u> pounding nails into boards. "Can I help?" he asked eagerly.

The <u>workers</u> laughed. "Your dad is our <u>employer</u>, and he would fire us if you got hurt. Don't worry! You'll be old enough to <u>work</u> before long. Then you'll wish you were still a boy with nothing to do but play."

The <u>workers</u> were right. When Jason turned 16 he began <u>working</u> for his dad's company. He worked very hard and tried to be the perfect <u>employee</u>. Sometimes when he was very tired, Jason remembered how he used to beg his dad to take him to <u>work</u> when he was a little boy.

BUILD

built
builder
building
builders

WORK

work
workers
working

EMPLOY

employed
employer
employee

ATTITUDE ADJUSTMENT

Harry has a bad attitude. He adds a negative prefix to almost everything he says. This is Harry's letter to you.

Dear Classmate,

I ~~dis~~like you because you are very ~~un~~kind to me. Your ~~un~~pleasant attitude makes me very ~~un~~happy.

I ~~dis~~like all of the other kids in my class, too. They are ~~un~~able to follow the rules in the games we play. This makes me quite ~~dis~~pleased. Their behavior is ~~in~~appropriate, and I am usually ~~un~~able to enjoy being in the class.

I really ~~dis~~like my teacher, Mr. Jones. He has ~~un~~realistic expectations of us, and I always ~~mis~~understand his directions. His explanations are ~~il~~logical, and I am ~~dis~~contented in his class.

I also ~~dis~~like my family, particularly my brother, Sam. His clothing is ~~dis~~tasteful and he always behaves ~~in~~appropriately. He is completely ~~un~~reliable, and that makes me feel very ~~un~~comfortable. I wish he would ~~dis~~appear sometime soon.

I especially ~~dis~~like my dog, Max. He has a very ~~un~~pleasant smell and looks ~~un~~appealing. Max is so ~~un~~intelligent that he is ~~in~~capable of doing tricks. Max is ~~dis~~loyal to me and ~~dis~~appears as soon as I come home from school each day. I really ~~dis~~agree that dogs are a man's best friend.

I am a very ~~un~~happy kid because I have the most ~~dis~~agreeable friends and the most ~~dis~~reputable family in the world.

~~In~~sincerely yours,

Harry

*Help give Harry an attitude adjustment! Delete the negative prefixes **un-, il-, in-,** and **dis-** from his letter. Read the letter again. Does Harry sound nicer without the negative prefixes?*

WORD TREE *

*This word tree has words from the Latin root **spect,** which means **look.** Can you figure out what the words mean by knowing the root? Fill in the root chart below:*

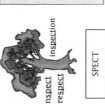

inspect
respect
inspection

SPECT

Root _spect_	Origin (Greek or Latin) _Latin_
Meaning of root _look_	
Word _inspect_	Meaning _look into or examine something_
Word _inspection_	Meaning _examination of something_
Word _respect_	Meaning _show high regard for someone_
Word _spectacles_	Meaning _glasses that help you see better_
Word _spectator_	Meaning _someone who watches an event_

Grow your own word trees using your Latin and Greek word lists. Underline the root in each word and find out what it means.

Root _form_	Origin (Greek or Latin) _Latin_
Meaning of root _shape_	
Word _inform_	Meaning _to tell about something important_
Word _information_	Meaning _important knowledge about something_
Word _formation_	Meaning _the way something is shaped_
Word _deformed_	Meaning _having an abnormal appearance_
Word _transform_	Meaning _to change the shape of something._

Root _bio_	Origin (Greek or Latin) _Greek_
Meaning of root _life_	
Word _biology_	Meaning _the study of living things_
Word _biography_	Meaning _the written history of a person's life_
Word _biographer_	Meaning _someone who writes the story of a person's life_
Word _biodiversity_	Meaning _the variety of living things_
Word _biodegradable_	Meaning _something that breaks down with the help of living things in the soil_

BE A ROOT DETECTIVE

Read the text below and underline the words with Latin and Greek roots. Give the meaning of each underlined word (use your Latin and Greek root lists if you need help). Then explain the meaning of the text in your own words.

The historian was inspecting the Native American artifacts that she had found in the cave. The first thing she did was photograph each item in its original location. Then she had to extract the items from the cave very carefully so that they wouldn't be damaged. Once the artifacts were removed from the cave, the historian needed a logical way to organize them. She carefully examined each item and used scientific techniques to decide how old it was. Every artifact was dated, except for some microscopic pieces of pottery that were too difficult to work with. Once the historian dated the artifacts, she began to put them in chronological order.

The historian took careful notes about the artifacts. She wrote a detailed description of each item in her journal and dictated additional notes into her tape recorder. She planned to return to the university and write a monograph about her discovery. She was very proud to have discovered such an incredible collection of ancient Native American artifacts.

Word _inspecting_	Origin (Greek or Latin) _Latin_	Meaning _examining something_
Word _artifacts_	Origin (Greek or Latin) _Latin_	Meaning _objects from a specific period_
Word _photograph_	Origin (Greek or Latin) _Greek_	Meaning _an image recorded by a camera_
Word _location_	Origin (Greek or Latin) _Latin_	Meaning _a specific place_
Word _extract_	Origin (Greek or Latin) _Latin_	Meaning _to draw out_
Word _techniques_	Origin (Greek or Latin) _Greek_	Meaning _methods of doing_
Word _microscopic_	Origin (Greek or Latin) _Greek_	Meaning _very small_
Word _description_	Origin (Greek or Latin) _Latin_	Meaning _giving a mental image of something_
Word _dictated_	Origin (Greek or Latin) _Latin_	Meaning _said orally to be recorded_
Word _monograph_	Origin (Greek or Latin) _Greek_	Meaning _a written record of a single thing_

The meaning of the paragraph in my own words: _(Answers will vary. Students should describe the historian's efforts to organize and record her findings.)_ (Extension activity for older or more advanced students: Have students list origins and meaning of other words with Latin and Greek roots in the above passage, such as historian and logical.)

185

BE A SUPER SLEUTH
Context Detective Work for Experts

How do you figure out the meaning of a word you aren't sure about? Look for the following clues that can help.

COMMA CLUES *are the easiest to figure out. The definition of the word is right there between the commas!*

EXPLANATION CLUES *can be a little more difficult when the definition is farther from the word it defines.*

FEELING CLUES *are challenging. You have to figure out the meaning of the word from all of the other information in the text.*

Look at each underlined word. Use context clues to figure out what the word means and then explain how you figured it out.

1. The Native American tribe settled on a <u>mesa</u>, a steep, flat-topped hill, hundreds of years ago. This location made the village difficult for ene-mies to attack.

   What does the word mean? <u>A steep, flat-topped hill</u>

   Type of clue <u>Comma clue; the word is defined in text within commas</u>

2. The colonists were forced to pay taxes they felt were unfair. The British government did not listen to their complaints. Some colonists were so angry they didn't want to be British citizens any more. They began to think of <u>rebelling</u> against Britain.

   What does the word mean? <u>Fighting back</u>

   Type of clue <u>Feeling clue; the text tells how the colonists were feeling</u>

3. Soon after the Revolutionary War Americans began to feel a sense of <u>nationalism</u>. They felt a sense of belonging to the new nation.

   What does the word mean? <u>Pride in being part of a nation</u>

   Type of clue <u>Explanation clue; the word is explained in the text</u>

BE A CONTEXT DETECTIVE

Context clues can be anywhere! Clues can be found next door, in the neighbor-hood, or far away. The easiest clues to find are the ones that are closest to the mystery word. But, even when clues are hard to find, good detectives don't give up! They keep on looking until they solve the mystery! (Mystery words are underlined.)

Here is an example of a **next-door** *clue:*

> The young <u>apprentice</u> was living with the printer's family and learning how to be a printer, too.

Notice how easy this clue is to find. It is right **next door** *(in the same sentence) as the mystery word.*

Explain the meaning of the mystery word: <u>Someone who learns a trade by working for an expert</u>

This is an example of an **in-the-neighborhood** *clue:*

> The ships were loaded with <u>exports</u> from the colonies. The ships sailed across the Atlantic Ocean on a trade route between Britain and the 13 colonies. Once the ships arrived in Britain, the products from the colonies were sold for a profit.

This clue is a little harder to find. It is **in the neighborhood,** *but you have to read more than one sentence to find the meaning of the mystery word.*

Explain the meaning of the mystery word: <u>Things that are sold and shipped to people in another place.</u>

Here is an example of a **far-away** *clue:*

> Plantation owners grew crops such as rice, tobacco, and <u>indigo</u>. These products were called cash crops because they brought money back to the plantation when they were sold. Large plantations were able to produce cash crops because they had so many slave workers.
> Indigo became an important cash crop in the 1700s. People liked colorful clothing. They were willing to spend more money for cloth that was dyed blue.

This clue requires good detective work! The meaning of the mystery word is **far away,** *in the next paragraph.*

Explain the meaning of the mystery word: <u>A plant that makes a blue dye</u>

How did you use clues to figure out each kind of mystery word? (Responses will vary; students should mention the use of next-door, in-the-neighborhood, and far-away clues.)

SEQUENCE SIGNAL WORDS

A **sequence chart** shows the most important things that happen in a story in the correct order. Fill in the sequence chart below with the most important things that happened in *Tale of a Tadpole*.

There is a tiny egg. → The tadpole comes out of the egg. → The tadpole swims in the pond. → The tadpole grows legs and arms. → The tadpole's tail shrinks. →

The tadpole becomes a frog.

A **cloze** is a story that is missing important words. This cloze is missing sequence words that help show the order of the events in the story. Read each sentence. Pick the correct sequence word or phrase from the box below, and write in on the line so that the story makes sense. (Each word/phrase is used only once.)

Now	Finally	Not long after that	Next	Then	First

This is how a tadpole becomes a frog.

First   there is a little egg in the pond.

Then   the little tadpole comes out of the egg.

Next   the tadpole grows legs and arms.

Not too long after that   , the tadpole's tail begins to shrink.

Finally   the tadpole becomes a little spotted frog.

Now   the frog can breathe air like we do.

Source: Wallace, 1988.

---

4. The Northwest Ordinance was passed in 1787. It was supposed to protect the rights of Native American tribes; however, this law did not work and the Native Americans continued to be pushed off of their land.

   What does the word mean?   Law

   Type of clue   Exploration clue; the word is explained in the text

5. The explorers often traveled on the Ohio River or one of its tributaries. It was much easier to travel on the many small rivers flowing from the Ohio than it was to travel through the wilderness in the new territory.

   What does the word mean?   Small rivers flowing from a big river

   Type of clue   Explanation clue; the word is explained in the text

6. There were many American settlers in Texas that wanted to be part of the United States. They wanted the government to annex Texas. Finally the government agreed, and Texas became a new state.

   What does the word mean?   Make a territory part of the country

   Type of clue   Explanation clue; the word is explained in the text

7. The new government helped people feel part of their country by choosing national symbols such as the American flag and the Great Seal of the United States.

   What does the word mean?   Something that stands for an important idea

   Type of clue   Explanation clue; the text gives examples that help explain

8. Textiles, cloth goods made from cotton or wool, were produced in large factories.

   What does the word mean?   Cloth goods made from cotton or wool

   Type of clue   Comma clue; the word is defined in the text within commas

Think about it!

Which sentences contain comma clues?   1,8

Which sentences contain explanation clues?   3–7

Which sentences contain feeling clues?   2

187

SIGNAL-WORDS CLOZE
Explorers and Settlers

*A **cloze** is a text that is missing key words. Read each sentence in the cloze passage below. Find the missing word or phrase in the box (each word/phrase is used only once). Write the word/phrase on the correct line so that the story makes sense.*

just like	but	alike	however	similar	different	yet

Explorers and settlers were ___similar___ because both groups came from Europe. Explorers were ___just like___ settlers because they did harmful things to the native people. ___However___ , explorers were ___different___ from settlers because they returned to Europe.

Explorers wanted to find riches and land for the king, ___but___ settlers wanted to find new homes. Explorers and settlers were ___alike___ in many ways, ___yet___ they had very different goals.

*Now, write your own **cloze**, using compare-and-contrast signal words. See if a friend can figure out the missing words.*

(Answers will vary. Cloze passages should contain compare-and-contrast signal words.)

_____
_____
_____
_____
_____
_____
_____

COMPARE AND CONTRAST SIGNAL WORDS
Explorers and Settlers

*A **Venn diagram** shows how two things are similar and different. Begin by filling in the middle section of the Venn diagram, showing how explorers and settlers were similar. Then fill in the outside circles, showing how explorers and settlers were different.*

Explorers   **Both**   **Settlers**

Explorers:
Men
Wanted riches
Wanted land for king
Returned to Europe

Both:
Came from Europe
Hurt native people

Settlers:
Families
Wanted freedom
Wanted new homes
Stayed in America

Before 1770, most goods— _such as_ clothing and shoes—were made by hand. _At that time_, most Americans lived on farms. A family member might need a shirt, _for example_ . _So_ , someone in the family would spin wool into thread, weave it into cloth, and sew the shirt.

Americans did not make all their own goods, _however_ . Some things—such as glass, tools, and some cloth—were made in Britain and imported. During the mid-1700s British inventors looked for ways to make these goods more cheaply and _thus_ increase their sales. (Armento et al., 1991, p. 422)

CAUSE-AND-EFFECT SIGNAL WORDS
The Little Red Hen

A **cause-and-effect** diagram shows the relationship between things that happen in a story or historical event. Let's look at the story "The Little Red Hen," for example. Write the causes (what the animals did to make the hen angry) in the first row of boxes. Then write the effect (what happened as a result) in the other box on the right.

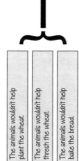

- The animals wouldn't help plant the wheat.
- The animals wouldn't help thresh the wheat.
- The animals wouldn't help bake the bread.

→ The hen ate the bread all by herself

Cause-and-effect cloze: *In the passage below, fill in the missing cause-and-effect signal words using words found in the box. (Each word/phrase is used only once.)*

| **because** | **therefore** | **as a result** | **consequently** | **so that** |

The hen asked the animals to help her plant the wheat _so that_ they could have bread. She asked them to help her harvest the wheat. They refused to help. _As a result_, the hen did it herself. She asked the animals to help her bake the bread. They would not help her. _Consequently_, the hen baked it herself. _Because_ she needed help and the animals would not help her, the hen got angry. _Therefore_, she ate the bread all by herself.

Think about the cause-and-effect signal words you used. Could you switch the signal words from one sentence to another? Why or why not?

You could switch signal words that mean the same thing (as a result, consequently, therefore). You can't switch signal words that mean different things (because, so that).

FIVE STEPS
Substitute a Synonym

Substitute a Synonym is a strategy that will help you figure out words you don't know. Look at this sentence:

A snowy owl named Hedwig **delivers** Harry Potter's mail.

Let's say you don't know the word **delivers.** Here are five steps that will help you make sense of the word.

FIVE STEPS

1. *Mine Your Memory and try to think of the word.* Have you seen it in a book or heard the word before?
2. *Try to picture the word in the sentence.* Imagine Hedwig flying into the room and dropping an envelope in Harry's hands.
3. *Think of other words that mean the same thing.* (**delivers**—gives, brings)
4. *Substitute a Synonym in the sentence.* A snowy owl named Hedwig **brings** Harry Potter's mail.
5. *Check! Does the synonym make sense in the sentence? If it makes sense, you can continue reading. If not, try again!* (Yes, the synonym makes sense.)

FIVE STEPS IN ACTION

Let's try it! We'll follow the five steps to make sense of the word **habitat** *in the following sentence:*

Hedwig lives with Harry Potter at Hogwarts, but snowy owls' normal habitat is in the Arctic region.

1. I think I remember reading about endangered animals' habitat—it's where they live.
2. I can picture the habitat: a cold, snowy place where snowy owls live.
3. *Habitat means a place where an animal lives, its home.*
4. Hedwig lives with Harry Potter at Hogwarts, but snowy owls' normal home is in the Arctic region.
5. Yes, it makes sense!

Now you try it! Follow the five steps to figure out the meaning of the under-lined words.

Hedwig looks small in her cage, but snowy owls have a 5-foot <u>wingspan</u>.

1. I think I've heard of wingspan before—how big the wings are.
2. I can picture Hedwig's wings spread out when she flies.
3. Wingspan is the distance across both wings.
4. ...but snowy owls have a 5-foot distance between their wings.
5. Yes, it makes sense.

When enemies <u>threaten</u> Hedwig, she knows how to defend herself.

1. I've heard of bad things threatening us.
2. I can picture a larger owl threatening Hedwig.
3. Threaten is to endanger (cause danger).
4. When enemies endanger Hedwig, she knows how to defend herself.
5. Yes, it makes sense.

Hedwig leaves her cage each night to hunt for <u>prey</u>.

1. I heard about prey and predators in science.
2. I can picture a mouse as an owl's prey.
3. Prey is something animals catch and eat.
4. Hedwig leaves her cage...to hunt for animals to catch and eat.
5. Yes, it makes sense.

Write four sentences of your own. Include a hard word in each sentence and underline it. Switch papers with a partner. Follow the five steps to figure out the meaning of the words in your partner's sentences.

1. (Responses will vary.)
2.
3.
4.

FEATURE ANALYSIS CHART
All About Reptiles

This feature analysis chart will help you organize information and learn new words about reptiles. Look at the example in the first row. The brontosaurus was enormous, is extinct, and was a vegetarian. So, those boxes are checked on the chart. Now look at the other rows and check each box that describes the reptile.

	enormous	extinct	endangered	vegetarian	carnivore	dangerous	poisonous
brontosaurus	✓	✓		✓			
tyrannosaurus	✓	✓			✓	✓	
rattlesnake					✓	✓	✓
Gila monster					✓	✓	✓
alligator					✓	✓	

FEATURE ANALYSIS CHART
In the Year of the Boar and Jackie Robinson

*This feature analysis chart will help you organize information and learn words from the book **In the Year of the Boar and Jackie Robinson,** by Bette Bao Lord. Each word that describes Shirley is checked (first row). Fill out the chart, checking the words that describe Mabel and Emily. Then fill in the chart, checking the words that describe you!*

	humiliated	formidable	obedient	progressive	brainy	ambassador	puny	persuasive
Shirley	✓		✓		✓	✓	✓	
Mabel		✓						✓
Emily				✓	✓			✓
You								

191

MORE WORD SCALES
Happy, Sad, and Big Words

*Brainstorm words to replace the simple, boring words **happy**, **sad**, and **big**, and put them in the box. Rank the words and put them on the word scales with the strongest word on top. Then use the strongest word in a sentence.*

(Answers may vary.)

The *Happy* Box

joyful · pleased
elated · overjoyed
delighted · ecstatic
pleased

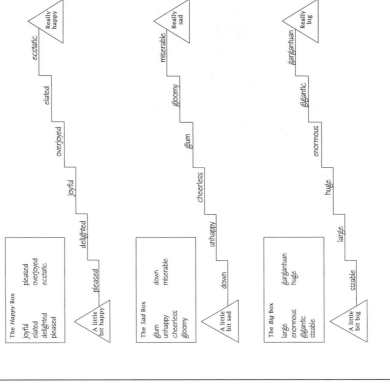

WORD SCALES
Mad and Bad Words

***Mom was mad.** How dull! **Mad** is a boring word that describes a range of feelings. The **Mad** Box below contains many strong, interesting words that mean **mad.** The words are ranked according to how much **madness** they express.*

The **Mad Box**   angry   furious   livid   annoyed   irritated   upset

*Now try the word **bad**. Brainstorm all of the words you can think of for **bad**. Write them in the Bad Box below.*

(Answers may vary.)

The **Bad Box**   evil   naughty   wicked   terrible   foul   obnoxious

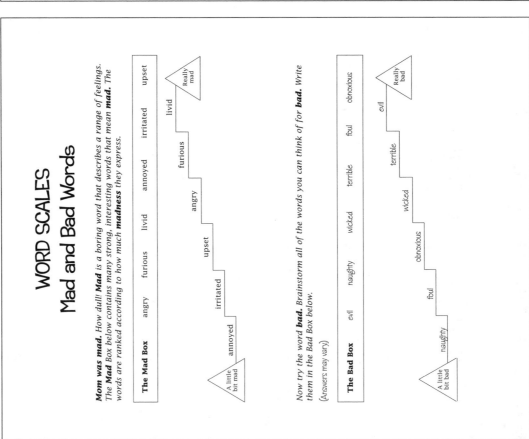

PICTURE PREDICTION RESPONSE CHART

In Search of a New World

Words I predict I'll find	Reason for my prediction
	(Answers may vary. See Figure 8.3 on p. 121 for a filled-out version of this page.)

PICTURE PREDICTION
The First Thanksgiving

Pictures give us clues about a story. They help us think about important words that the author will use to tell the story. Look at the picture below. What important words do you predict will be in the story? How can you tell—what is the reason for your prediction?

Words I predict I'll find	The reason for my prediction
Native American	You can see a Native American in the picture.
pilgrim	You can see pilgrims in the picture.
Thanksgiving	It looks like the beginning of Thanksgiving.
hungry	The pilgrims didn't have enough to eat.
starving	If they were really hungry, they might have been starving.
food	The pilgrims needed food if they were hungry.
turkey	We eat turkey at Thanksgiving.

Read the story below. Circle the words that you predicted would be in the story.

In the year 1620 the (Pilgrims) sailed on the Mayflower. They had planned to arrive in Virginia, but they landed in Massachusetts instead. It was a difficult journey to the new place the (Pilgrims) called Plymouth Colony.

It was icy cold in Massachusetts that winter. The (Pilgrims) did not have enough to eat and were very (hungry.) They survived the first winter thanks to the Wampanoag Indians. The (Pilgrims) and the Wampanoag signed a peace treaty and promised to be friends. The (Native Americans) brought the settlers warm blankets and gifts of (food,) including corn and wild (turkey.) The (Pilgrims) celebrated their survival with the holiday of (Thanksgiving.)

Check to see how many of the words you predicted are in the text. What important words would you add to your list? Write the words in the chart below and explain why they are important.

More important words	Why these word are important
celebrate	They celebrated Thanksgiving.
survival	The pilgrims lived through winter.
treaty	The pilgrims made friends with the Native Americans.

CATCH A COGNATE WORKSHEET

*Many of the words we use in school are similar in Spanish and English. For example, the word **similar** is exactly the same in both languages. Use the Catch a Cognate Cue Card to help you figure out if an unknown word is a cognate. Here is an example: **Her heart beat rapidly after running to class.***

1. **Look and listen.** Look at the word rapidly. Does it look like a word you know in Spanish? Does it *sound* like a Spanish word? Could it be a cognate?
   Rapidly looks and sounds a lot like the word rápida in Spanish.

2. **Consider it.** Do you know what the word means in Spanish?
   The word rápida in Spanish means fast.

3. **Try it.** Read the whole sentence using the Spanish word instead of the word in English.
   Her heart beat was rápida after running to class.

4. **Think about it.** Does the word make sense in a sentence?
   Yes, rápido makes sense in the sentence. I think it's a cognate!

Work with a partner and find each of the English cognates for the Spanish words in parentheses. Follow the steps on the Catch a Cognate Cue Card.

1. The cave paintings were made by prehistoric people. (*prehistórico*)
2. Discuss the characteristics of the people in the New England colonies. (*características*)
3. What is the correct abbreviation for the state of California? (*abreviatura*)
4. Find the congruent shapes. (*congruente*)
5. Write the definition of each word. (*definición*)

With your partner, identify cognates for the underlined words using the Catch a Cognate Cue Card.

1. Explain how the system works.   *sistema*
2. Combine these numbers.   *combinar*
3. Describe the character in the story.   *describir*
4. What does this symbol mean?   *símbolo*
5. Give biographical information about yourself.   *biografía*

Write some sentences of your own, using words that are cognates. Give your sentences to a friend and ask him or her to catch your cognates. (Responses will vary; a few examples are shown.)

I like to study history (*historia*)

What is your favorite color? (*color, favorito*)

I want to study biology (*biología*)

We are going to visit Spain. (*visitar*)

Index

Page numbers followed by *f* indicate figures; those followed by *t* indicate tables.

Mine Your Memory strategy
  in Clarifying Strategy Decision Tree, 94
  cue cards, 38, 157
  with English language learners, 147–148
  overview, 20–21
  Spanish translation, 157
  teaching vignettes, 21, 23–24, 64, 82
  with young children, 136–137, 141
Modeling
  research study at elementary school, 168–169
  Stop Sign activity, 73–76
  as teaching strategy, 61
  teaching vignettes, 62–67
Monitoring, see Self-monitoring
Morphological support
  defined, 181
  evaluating, 100, 101t
Motivating children, 4–5

National Reading Panel report, 8
Native language poetry, 153–154
Negative prefixes
  Attitude Adjustment exercise, 24, 42
  frequency of, 22
  teaching vignette, 23–24
  word lists, 41
Neruda, Pablo, poetry of, 154
Non-English speakers, see English language learners;
    Spanish-speaking children
Notes, see Place a Post-It strategy

Opposition clues
  Consider the Context strategy, 35, 58
  signal words, 31t, 32
  Stop for Signal Words activity, 57

Phonics instruction, 145–146, 147–148
Picture Prediction activities
  with English language learners, 146–147
  overview, 116–118, 119
  in read-aloud programs, 134
  sample worksheet, 129
  teaching vignettes, 118–119, 120–122
Picture Prediction Response Chart, 121f, 130
Place a Post-It strategy
  in Clarifying Strategy Decision Tree, 94
  cue card, 37, 38
  Spanish translation, 157
Poetry
  native language poetry, 153–154
  to stimulate imagination, 106
  teaching vignette, 3–4
  writing, as instructional method, 107–108
Post-it notes, see Place a Post-It strategy
Practice, guiding, 61, 180
Prediction exercises, see Word prediction
Prefixes
  defined, 181
  negative prefixes, 22, 23–24, 41, 42
  prefix chart, 40
  in Root Webs activity, 24, 25, 25f
Prereading activities
  Picture Prediction, 117–118, 134, 146–147
  providing background knowledge, 30
  in read-aloud programs, 134
Primary grades, see Young children; specific grades

Procedural knowledge
  as basis for vocabulary instruction, 9, 13f
  defined, 13, 181
  scope and sequence of instruction, 172f

Reading
  children's views of, 73
  emphasis on fluency, 73, 135
  read-aloud programs, 134–135
  reading failure, defined, 181
  relationship to vocabulary, 8, 9–10, 9f, 166, 170–171
  self-regulation and, 7
  as series of pictures, 71, 74, 105
  speed of, 79
Red-light words, 77, 78f
Regulation, see Self-regulation
Repeated read-aloud programs, 134–135
Research study, at elementary school, 167–170
Romance languages, 149
  see also Spanish-speaking children
Root Webs activity, 24–26, 25f, 26f
Roots
  Be a Root Detective exercise, 28, 47
  defined, 181
  Greek roots, 26–27, 44
  high-frequency roots, 27
  Latin roots, 26–27, 43

Scaffolding, 61, 181
Schoolwide programs, 170–171, 172f, 173
Second grade
  instructional strategies, 172f
  teaching vignettes, 97, 140–141
Self-monitoring
  defined, 181
  grade-level instructional sequence, 172f
  in metacognition, 72
  as recommended strategy, 8
  teaching vignette, 73–76
Self-regulation
  clarifying strategies for, 89–93
  defined, 181
  grade-level instructional sequence, 172f
  influence on reading comprehension, 7
  internalizing, 71
  in metacognition, 72
  as recommended strategy, 8, 9
Semantic feature analysis, 114–116, 125, 126
Semantic maps, 113–114, 114f
Sentences, using words in, 11
  see also Substitute a Synonym
Sequence signal words, 31–32, 31t, 52, 56
Signal words
  cause-and-effect signal words, 31t, 32–33, 55
  cloze activity, 32, 54
  compare-and-contrast words, 31t, 32
  high-frequency words, 31, 31t
  sequence signal words, 31–32, 31t, 52, 56
  Stop for Signal Words activity, 33–35, 56–57
Sixth grade
  root lists, 27
  teaching vignettes, 23–24, 89–91, 92–93
  words with negative prefixes, 41
Skipping words, caution against, 37, 72
Snapshot exercise, 28, 48